Simply Delicious
& *Surprisingly Healthy* Cookbook

Simply Delicious
& *Surprisingly Healthy* Cookbook

Published by Julie Terrell, Louisville, Kentucky.

Printed in the United States.

For information about purchasing bulk copies, please contact:
Julie Terrell
www.julieterrell.com

Designed by Alfred Moreschi

Cover photograph by Dean Lavenson
taken at The Trend Companies of Kentucky, Louisville, Kentucky

acknowledgements

First and foremost, I was inspired to write this book for you. I am a firm believer that God gives us talents and it is our responsibility to cultivate and share them. It is my intention to provide a cookbook that is an educational tool, as well as one that satisfies and nourishes your body.

The body is the temple and the only one that we will inhabit in our lifetime. If we expect to live a good quality of life, we must take the necessary measures to make that possible. With that in mind, we are human beings and are not designed to endure complete deprivation. I think you will find that these recipes are manageable and a delicious alternative to traditional favorites. In love and peace....

I would like to dedicate this book to my mother Mary and my brother Scott. Words could never express the love, admiration, and respect that I have for you. Thank you for being you. I love you.

My nephews Hunter, Jacob and Rhett, you bring so much joy to my life.

My stepsister Missy, the miles may separate us, but you are in my heart.

My stepfather Wayne, you are truly my friend.

My Grandpa Chanely and Grandma Terrell, I have a great appreciation for your wisdom. Grandpa, thank you for the delicious vegetables that you grow each year! I love you both.

I am a very fortunate soul to have so many beautiful people in my life. The following will express my sincere appreciation.

Melodie, across the miles that separate us, I have never had a day that I knew you were not with me. I feel you strongly, even though you are not always present. Without you, my life would have been incomplete. You are so special to me. Thank you for being my friend.

Kim, the sweet childlike innocence that we share... You ground me. There is no one like you. Thank you for being my friend.

Julie, Dawn and Lauren, your friendships have encouraged me to be my best! Thank you for your undying support, loyalty, and for believing in me. But most of all, thank you for being my friends!

My extended family, where would I be without all of you!

To my clients, each and every one of you inspire me. I am so grateful to be a part of your world! I love you all!

In memory of my cat Gillian and dog Midas, rest in peace 2006. They were two of my greatest teachers of unconditional love.

I would like to thank the following companies for their support.

My thanks are extended to Nancy Miller of Miller and Madison Company. Your expertise and guidance have been invaluable to me.

Al Moreschi, for the graphic design of the book.

Dean Lavenson, for the cover photography.

Trend Appliances, for providing the set for the cover of the book.

Julie Terrell

about the book

My life's journey has taken me places I would have never imagined. I spent my adolescent years in Louisville where I dabbled in modeling and pageantry. I was in my second year of college when I was offered an opportunity of a lifetime. I moved to Philadelphia and began a career as a flight attendant with an international carrier. Traveling had always been a dream of mine. The exposure to different countries, cultures and people was an education within itself and provided me with an enormous opportunity for personal growth. I enjoyed these careers for many years. Eventually, I moved home to Louisville.

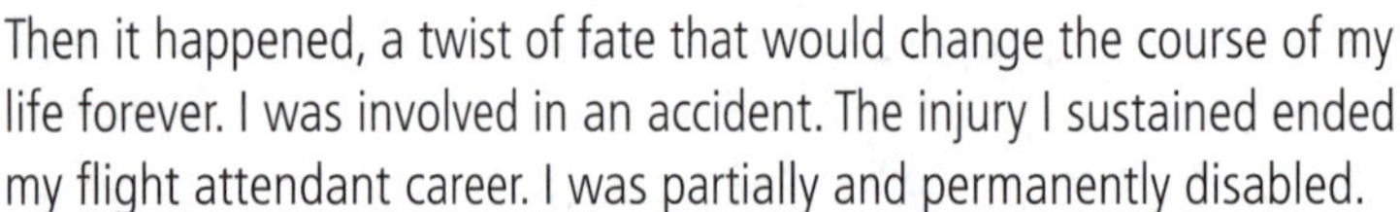

Then it happened, a twist of fate that would change the course of my life forever. I was involved in an accident. The injury I sustained ended my flight attendant career. I was partially and permanently disabled. In an effort to regain some mobility, I spent four years recovering from three painful surgeries, physical therapy, muscle atrophy, weight gain and, even worse, depression. There were four things that saved me during this difficult time. The first was my faith in God to lead me in the right direction. The second was the loving support of my mother who nursed me back to health in more ways than one. The third was exercise, and last but not least, my love for cooking. I spent countless hours in the gym rebuilding my body and learning to embrace my disability, not allowing it to define me. Meanwhile, I was busy in the kitchen modifying traditional recipes and putting a healthy spin on them. I began researching the nutritional content found in foods and discovered how a healthy diet can actually heal the body and prevent disease. By simply developing an exercise regimen and altering my diet, my body healed itself to the best of its ability. What a concept! I slowly began to realize out of self preservation, a whole new world was presenting itself to me through the guise of my disability. My disability was actually a gift and it inspired me to further my education in fitness and nutrition.

It is now a responsibility or a calling to share my experience in an effort to help educate and heal other people. I am now a certified personal fitness trainer, a certified dietary supplement specialist, a certified specialist in performance nutrition, a resistance training specialist, a certified CORE fitness instructor, and I am in management at a state of the art fitness facility. I have a regular cooking and nutrition segment on a television show and write a regular nutrition column in a regional magazine. I also do cooking demonstrations for various events, as well as public speaking. My latest ventures are my company Flex Appeal, LLC and last but not least, this cookbook.

I am honored to have the unique opportunity to inspire, motivate and educate people who may have similar circumstances or simply want to improve their quality of life. This is truly a blessing and the greatest gift I have ever been given!

Please visit my website: www.julieterrell.com

Julie Terrell

contents

contents continued

Pasta and Grains

Seafood

Side Dishes

Vegetarian and Vegan

Dressings and Sauces

Desserts

appetizers

Black Bean Salsa

Allow the beans to marinate for the best flavor. This is an excellent complement to the Homemade Tortilla Chips (See recipe page 6)

One 15-ounce can black beans, rinsed and drained
½ cup red bell pepper, chopped
¼ cup corn
8 ounce can of diced tomatoes
⅓ cup red onion, chopped
½ cup fresh cilantro, minced
3 tablespoons lime juice
1 tablespoon canola oil
1 tablespoon white wine vinegar
1 tablespoon reduced sodium soy sauce
1 packet Splenda
2 teaspoons chili powder
1 teaspoon garlic powder
Salt and pepper to taste

In a large bowl, combine the beans, red pepper, corn, tomatoes, onion and cilantro. Set aside. In a small bowl, mix the lime juice, oil, vinegar, soy sauce, Splenda, chili powder, garlic powder, salt and pepper. Pour the mixture over the beans and marinate at room temperature for two hours or until ready to serve.

Nutrition Facts
(Per Serving)

Calories 121
Fat Calories 21
Total Fat 2.3g
Saturated Fat 0.2g
Cholesterol 0mg
Sodium 187mg
Total Carbs 19g
Fiber 6.1g
Protein 5.8g

Did You Know…

- Beans contain more protein than any other plant-derived food.
- Beans are high in soluble fiber. Soluble fiber is important when trying to control blood cholesterol levels.
- Beans are a great choice for diabetics because their balance of complex carbohydrates and protein provides a slow, steady source of glucose. This is better than the sudden surge that can occur after eating simple carbohydrates.

Deviled Eggs

Makes 24 eggs

Nutrition Facts
(Per Serving)

Calories	39
Fat Calories	27
Total Fat	2.9g
Saturated Fat	0.7g
Cholesterol	81mg
Sodium	43mg
Total Carbs	0.6g
Fiber	0g
Protein	2.4g

Did You Know...

- Eggs are a nutritional powerhouse. They are a great source of protein and vitamin B12, which is essential for nerve function.
- Eggs are a great source of the antioxidants Zeaxanthin and Lutein. These powerful antioxidants may reduce the risk of macular degeneration which is a leading cause of blindness.
- Eggs are considered a complete protein as they contain 20 different amino acids; 9 of these cannot be manufactured by the body and are considered essential. These 9 essential amino acids must come from food alone.

12 free-range eggs
4 tablespoons reduced fat mayonnaise
1 teaspoon yellow mustard
1 tablespoon Splenda
1 teaspoon paprika
1 teaspoon fresh flat leaf parsley, chopped

Boil the eggs, with a pinch of salt, for 20 minutes. The salt will ensure the eggs are easier to peel. Drain the eggs and let them cool for 30 minutes. Then, crack the eggs and remove the outer shell. Cut the eggs in half and place the yolks in a food processor. The food processor is an invaluable tool to ensure the yolk mixture becomes smooth and creamy. Place the egg whites in a dish and refrigerate. Add the mayonnaise, yellow mustard and Splenda to the yolks in the food processor and blend for one minute until the desired texture is achieved. Remove the egg whites from the refrigerator and spoon the mixture into the whites. Sprinkle paprika and parsley on top of the eggs to garnish. Refrigerate until ready to serve.

Fresh Tomato and Basil Bruschetta

Makes 24 appetizers

1 loaf of whole grain bread (prepared)
6 Roma tomatoes, diced (about 1 pound)
½ medium red onion (about ½ cup), coarsely chopped
½ cup snipped fresh basil leaves
3 garlic cloves, minced
2 teaspoons balsamic vinegar
¼ teaspoon olive oil
1 teaspoon lemon juice
¼ teaspoon salt
Cracked black pepper to taste
¼ cup black olives, chopped
¼ cup grated fresh Parmesan cheese

Preheat the oven to 350°F. Arrange the bread slices on a flat baking pan. Bake 10-12 minutes or until light golden brown.

In a small bowl, combine the tomatoes, red onion, basil, garlic, vinegar, oil, lemon juice, salt, cracked black pepper, and black olives; mix gently. Spoon the tomato mixture over the bread slices. Sprinkle with Parmesan cheese. Serve immediately.

Nutrition Facts
(Serving size 2 appetizers)

Calories	94
Fat Calories	16
Total Fat	1.8g
Saturated Fat	0.6g
Cholesterol	2mg
Sodium	230mg
Total Carbs	15.8g
Fiber	2.6g
Protein	3.8g

Did You Know…

- Whole grain bread is a good source of complex carbohydrates that are rated lower on the glycemic index.
- Whole grain bread is higher in fiber and is a good source of niacin, riboflavin, and other B complex vitamins.
- Lycopene is in the skin of tomatoes and is fat soluble. Add a little olive oil to the tomatoes and the oil increases absorption of the lycopene.
- Onions contain flavonoids that may prevent or protect against lung cancer.

Holy Guacamole

Serves 6-8

Nutrition Facts	
1 serving is 2.2 oz.	
Calories	118
Fat Calories	10g
Total Fat	10g
Saturated Fat	1.5g
Cholesterol	0
Sodium	33mg
Total Carbs	5.6g
Fiber	3.1g
Protein	1.4g

Did You Know...

- Avocados are a rich source of folate, vitamin A and potassium. They also have useful amounts of protein, iron, and magnesium.
- Onions have a mild anti-bacterial effect that may help prevent superficial infections.
- Tomatoes are a good source of lycopene, an antioxidant that may prevent certain cancers.

2 ripe avocadoes, cored and peeled
2 tablespoons lime juice
1 tablespoon jalapeños
¼ cup cilantro, chopped
Salt and pepper to taste
¼ cup red onion, chopped
¼ cup tomatoes, chopped

Combine avocadoes, lime juice, jalapeños, cilantro, and salt and pepper in a food processor. Blend until almost smooth. Remove contents from food processor and place in a bowl. Add red onion and tomatoes to the contents of the bowl. Mix thoroughly and refrigerate.

Homemade Tortilla Chips

Serves 10

6 whole wheat tortillas
1 tablespoon garlic powder
olive oil spray
¼ cup fresh flat leaf parsley, minced
1 teaspoon sea salt
Cracked black pepper to taste

Preheat the oven to 400°. Stack the tortillas and cut into triangles. Spray a large flat baking sheet with olive oil and place the tortillas flat on the sheet. Spray the tortillas with olive oil and sprinkle on the garlic, parsley, salt and pepper. Bake 7 - 10 minutes or until brown. Let stand and serve at room temperature.

Nutrition Facts
(Per Serving)

Calories	114
Fat Calories	72
Total Fat	7.9g
Saturated Fat	1.3g
Cholesterol	0mg
Sodium	308mg
Total Carbs	9g
Fiber	1g
Protein	1.6g

Did You Know...

- Whole wheat is low in fat and high in nutritional value as opposed to white flour tortillas.
- Olive oil is noted for the good or healthier fats found in our diets.
- Parsley is very rich in chlorophyll and carotenes. It is also a great source of vitamin C, iron and folic acid.

Hummus

Hummus is a very popular dish in the Mediterranean diet. It is a great food choice for vegetarians and is delicious when used as a condiment.

Makes 2 cups

Nutrition Facts (Per Serving)
Calories 183
Fat Calories 123
Total Fat 13.8
Saturated Fat 1.8g
Cholesterol 0mg
Sodium 334mg
Total Carbs 12.5g
Fiber 2.7g
Protein 2.5g

One 16 ounce can chick peas, drained
½ cup olive oil
One 8 ounce can black olives, drained
3 medium garlic cloves, minced
2 tablespoons fresh lemon juice
Parsley, for garnish
1 teaspoon salt

Drain the chick peas and black olives and place them in a food processor. Pour in the olive oil. Add the garlic cloves, lemon juice and salt. Pulse until the texture is smooth. Refrigerate. Garnish with parsley.

Did You Know…

- Beans contain more protein than any other plant derived food.
- Beans are a good source of starch, B complex, iron, potassium, zinc and other essential minerals.
- Beans are high in soluble fiber and low in fat.
- Beans are nutritional powerhouses that may also control cholesterol levels.
- Garlic may prevent or fight certain cancers.
- Garlic may alleviate nasal congestion.
- Garlic may help lower high blood pressure and elevated blood cholesterol.

Mediterranean Bean Dip

Homemade Tortilla Chips (See recipe page 6)
One 15-ounce can garbanzo beans
3 tablespoons tahini (sesame-seed paste)
¼ cup lemon juice
1 teaspoon ground cumin
½ tsp sea salt
1 clove garlic, minced
¾ cup plain nonfat organic yogurt
½ cup cucumber, sliced
½ cup radishes, sliced
1/3 cup tomatoes, diced
¼ cup crumbled feta cheese
1 tablespoon oregano
Black cracked peppercorn (to taste)

Prepare Homemade Tortilla Chips and set aside.

Drain the beans, reserving ¼ cup of the liquid, and then rinse beans. In a food processor, blend the beans, the reserved liquid, tahini, lemon juice, cumin, salt and garlic until smooth. Spoon the mixture onto a shallow platter and spread evenly. Spread the yogurt over the bean mixture. Sprinkle cucumber, radishes, tomatoes, feta, oregano, and pepper over the yogurt. Tuck the Homemade Tortilla Chips around the edge of the platter. Serve cold.

Makes 10 servings

Nutrition Facts
(Per Serving)

Calories	107
Fat Calories	33
Total Fat	3.7g
Saturated Fat	1g
Cholesterol	3mg
Sodium	303mg
Total Carbs	13.9g
Fiber	2.5g
Protein	4.6g

Did You Know…

- Beans are a great source of starch.
- Most beans are high in soluble fiber.
- Yogurt is an excellent source of calcium and phosphorus. Yogurt provides useful amounts of vitamin A, several B vitamins, and zinc.
- Cucumbers are very low in calories and contain mostly water.
- Radishes have a fair source of vitamin C, are low in calories and are high in fiber.

Potato Skins

Makes 16 appetizers

Nutrition Facts
(Per Serving)

Calories	50
Fat Calories	20
Total Fat	2.2g
Saturated Fat	0.8g
Cholesterol	6mg
Sodium	132mg
Total Carbs	4.4g
Fiber	0.8g
Protein	3.2g

Did You Know...

- Red potatoes are a good source of vitamins C, B6, potassium and other minerals.
- Red potatoes are high in complex carbohydrates and fiber and are also rated lower on the glycemic index.
- Yogurt is an excellent source of calcium and contains protein.
- Yogurt may be a good choice for people who are sensitive to lactose.
- Cheese is a great source of calcium.

16 small red potatoes, scrubbed
½ cup grated Parmesan cheese
½ cup plain low-fat organic yogurt
3 tablespoons green onion or chives, chopped
⅓ cup turkey bacon, crumbled
½ teaspoon paprika

Preheat the oven to 375°. Scrub the potatoes and pierce each potato in several areas with a fork. Arrange the potatoes in a single layer in a shallow baking pan. Bake approximately 1 hour, until tender when pierced with a fork. Let the potatoes stand and cool.

In a small bowl, mix the cheese, yogurt, and onion or chives. Cut the potatoes in half and scoop out some of the flesh. Fill in the hollowed areas with the yogurt mixture. Bake in the oven at 350° for another ten minutes. Remove and sprinkle on the turkey bacon and paprika. Serve warm.

Roasted Garlic Aioli with a Hint of Basil

Makes ¾ cup

- 1 head garlic, separated into cloves
- 1½ tablespoons extra virgin olive oil
- ¼ cup reduced-fat mayonnaise
- 3 tablespoons organic plain nonfat yogurt
- 1 tablespoon fresh basil, chopped
- Sea salt to taste

Preheat the oven to 450°. Trim the tips off the garlic cloves, and remove the skins. Place the cloves in aluminum foil. Drizzle with olive oil and sprinkle with sea salt. Wrap the garlic completely in the foil, sealing well. Roast in the oven for 25 - 30 minutes until the garlic is soft. Place the garlic and the mayonnaise in a food processor and blend for 30 - 60 seconds. Stir in the yogurt and basil, and mix thoroughly. Cover and refrigerate.

Nutrition Facts
(Per Serving)

Calories	82
Fat Calories	60
Total Fat	6.7g
Saturated Fat	0.9g
Cholesterol	3mg
Sodium	171mg
Total Carbs	4.9g
Fiber	0.1g
Protein	0.7g

Did You Know…

- Garlic has been associated with reducing the risk of colorectal and prostate cancers.
- Garlic contains high concentrations of the trace minerals selenium and germanium.
- By chopping or crushing garlic, an important compound, Allicin, is released. Many of garlic's health benefits are attributed to Allicin.

Shrimp Cocktail

Serves 4-6

Nutrition Facts (Per Serving)	
Calories	220
Fat Calories	24
Total Fat	2.8g
Saturated Fat	0.5g
Cholesterol	213mg
Sodium	307mg
Total Carbs	19.2g
Fiber	1g
Protein	29.8g

Did You Know...

- Shrimp is an excellent source of selenium, vitamin B12 and lean protein.
- Many types of seafood, including shrimp, have been shown to aid in the prevention of heart disease, cancer and Alzheimer's disease.
- Shrimp has higher amounts of cholesterol than many other fish.

1¼ pounds fresh large shrimp, shell on
2 tablespoons Old Bay Seasoning

Cocktail Sauce

Yields 1¼ cups

1 cup ketchup
2 - 3 tablespoons prepared horseradish
2 tablespoons fresh lemon juice
1 teaspoon capers, drained
2 tablespoons Worcestershire sauce

Rinse the shrimp, with the shells on, in a colander. Place the shrimp in a saucepan with 3 cups of water and the Old Bay seasoning. Bring the water to a boil and cover. Steam the shrimp for 5 minutes or until they have turned pink. Drain the shrimp and let cool. Once the shrimp have cooled, remove the outer shell while preserving the tail. To remove the vein, use a knife to cut along the backside of the shrimp from the head to the tail. While deveining the shrimp, rinse with cool water. Set aside and chill.

For the Cocktail Sauce: Place the ketchup, horseradish, lemon juice, capers and Worcestershire sauce in a mixing bowl and blend together. Serve the shrimp chilled with the Cocktail Sauce.

Simply Salsa

This salsa is fresh and very easy to prepare.

4 ripe tomatoes or one 8 ounce can tomatoes
½ Spanish onion, coarsely chopped
2 - 3 tablespoons fresh cilantro, chopped (optional)
1 - 2 tablespoons fresh lime juice
1 tablespoon jalapeños, diced
1 - 2 tablespoons green chilies, diced
Salt and pepper to taste

Combine tomatoes, onion, cilantro, lime juice, jalapeños, green chilies, and salt and pepper in a food processor and pulse. Remove the salsa from the processor and place in a bowl. Refrigerate immediately.

Makes 2 cups (about 6 servings)

Nutrition Facts
Serving Size: ¼ Cup

Calories	12
Fat Calories	0.5
Total Fat	0.1
Cholesterol	0g
Sodium	5mg
Total Carbs	3g
Fiber	0.5g
Protein	0.5g

Did You Know…

- Tomatoes are a useful source of vitamin C, beta carotene, folate and potassium.
- Onions may lower elevated blood cholesterol levels and blood pressure.
- Onions' sulfur compounds may block carcinogens.
- Chiles are an excellent source of beta carotene and vitamin C. They may also help prevent nasal congestion.
- Chiles may prevent blood clots that can lead to a heart attack or stroke.
- Lime is an excellent source of vitamin C.

Smoked Salmon Bites

Serves 2

Nutrition Facts (Per Serving)	
Calories	132
Fat Calories	35
Total Fat	3.9g
Saturated Fat	0.8g
Cholesterol	21mg
Sodium	2017mg
Total Carbs	7.6g
Fiber	2.1g
Protein	16.6g

Did You Know…

- Salmon is rich in Omega 3 fatty acids. It is also rich in vitamin B12, potassium and selenium.
- Salmon is an excellent source of protein.
- Dill may aid in the de-toxification process of the liver.
- Rye bread is high in fiber. As a result, rye has been useful in reducing the symptoms of irritable bowel syndrome.

This is a light dish that is very satisfying when eaten as a snack

6 ounces smoked salmon
½ fresh lemon, juiced
2 tablespoons capers
1 tablespoon fresh dill
1 tablespoon red onion, diced (optional)
6 small rye bread rounds

Spread the bread on a serving dish. Place one ounce of the salmon on each bread round. Sprinkle the capers, dill, and red onion on the salmon. Drizzle with fresh lemon juice. Serve chilled.

Swedish Meatballs

This is a great appetizer for a party!

Makes about 20-25 meatballs

Meatballs

1¼ pounds 93% lean ground turkey
1 teaspoon onion powder
1 egg white
¼ cup seasoned dry whole wheat bread crumbs
1 teaspoon dried oregano
1 garlic clove, pressed
½ teaspoon salt
Pepper to taste

Sauce

1 can (8 ounces) jellied cranberry sauce
¼ cup ketchup
¼ cup orange marmalade
¼ cup Splenda brown sugar
1 tablespoon Worcestershire sauce
Salt and pepper to taste (optional)

In a food processor, combine the turkey, onion, egg white, bread crumbs, oregano, garlic, salt and pepper. Blend for one minute.

Shape the meat mixture into meatballs; place the meatballs in a crock pot. Meanwhile, in a small bowl, combine the cranberry sauce, ketchup, marmalade, Splenda brown sugar and Worcestershire sauce, and mix well. Pour the sauce over the meatballs, and mix gently to evenly coat the meatballs. Simmer 4 - 6 hours. Add salt and pepper to taste. Stir gently before serving.

Nutrition Facts

Serving Size: 4 meatballs

Calories 266
Fat Calories 73
Total Fat 8.1g
Saturated Fat 2.2g
Cholesterol 75mg
Sodium 573mg
Total Carbs 30.5g
Fiber 0.9g
Protein 17.9g

Did You Know…

- Turkey is an excellent source of protein.
- Turkey is a good source of vitamin A, the B vitamins, and minerals.
- Cranberries are a fair source of vitamin C and fiber.
- Cranberries also contain bioflavonoids, thought to protect eyesight and help prevent cancer.

Tomatillo Salsa

**Makes 2 cups
(about 6 servings)**

Nutrition Facts
(Per Serving)

Calories	38
Fat Calories	8
Total Fat	1g
Saturated Fat	0g
Cholesterol	0mg
Sodium	204mg
Total Carbs	7g
Fiber	0g
Protein	1g

Did You Know...

- Tomatoes are a rich source of vitamin C, which is found in the jelly substance encasing the seeds.
- Onions may lower blood cholesterol and blood pressure. Onions also have an antibacterial effect.
- Limes are a rich source of vitamin C.
- Red peppers are a great source of Beta Carotene and vitamin C.

1 pound tomatillos
1 cup onion, coarsely chopped
2 garlic cloves, peeled and coarsely chopped
1 tablespoon jalapeño peppers, coarsely chopped
1 tablespoon green chilies
½ teaspoon sea salt
½ cup cilantro, chopped
2 tablespoons lime juice
Pinch of sugar and white pepper

Remove the papery brown husks from the tomatillos. Place in a saucepan, cover with water, and bring to a boil. Reduce the heat to medium and cook, uncovered, until just tender, about 5 minutes. Drain and rinse under cold running water to avoid overcooking. In a food processor, combine the tomatillos, onion, garlic, jalapeños, chilies, and salt. Pulse, until the mixture becomes a textured purée. Add the cilantro and lime juice and pulse again, about 30 seconds. Then, add a pinch of sugar and white pepper. Stir and serve at room temperature.

Tomato Basil Boats with Fresh Mozzarella

Serves 8

8 Roma tomatoes
⅔ cup extra virgin olive oil
¼ cup balsamic vinegar
2 tablespoons garlic, minced
Salt and pepper to taste
½ cup fresh basil (leaves intact)
1 pound fresh mozzarella balls

Cut the tomatoes in half. Scoop out the inside and discard. Place the tomato boats in a serving dish. Drizzle the tomatoes with extra virgin olive oil and balsamic vinegar. Sprinkle the garlic and salt and pepper over the tomato boats. Place one basil leaf inside each boat and top with one mozzarella ball.

Nutrition Facts
(Per Serving)

Calories	200
Fat Calories	120
Total Fat	14.2g
Saturated Fat	8.8g
Cholesterol	50mg
Sodium	240mg
Total Carbs	5.2g
Fiber	0.8g
Protein	12.8g

Did You Know…

- Tomatoes are rich in vitamin C, beta carotene, folate, and potassium.
- Tomatoes are a great source of lycopene, an antioxidant which is found in the skin of the tomatoes.
- Olive oil contains essential fatty acids which are needed for hormone production.
- Olive oil makes it possible for the absorption of fat soluble vitamins A, D, E and K.
- Cheese is high in protein and calcium. It is also a great source of vitamin B12.

Tomato and Corn Relish

Serves 8

Nutrition Facts	
Serving Size: About ½ cup	
Calories	86
Fat Calories	7
Total Fat	0.8g
Saturated Fat	0.1g
Cholesterol	0mg
Sodium	322mg
Total Carbs	17.2g
Fiber	2.6g
Protein	2.7g

Did You Know...

- Corn is a good source of fiber and essential fatty acids.
- Corn may help to protect against heart disease.
- Consuming red peppers may help to protect against cataracts.

One16-ounce can corn kernels, drained
One 28-ounce can whole tomatoes, drained, seeded, and chopped
½ cup red onion, chopped
½ cup sweet red pepper, diced
¼ cup fresh lemon juice
1 teaspoon Splenda
1 tablespoon jalapeño pepper, seeded and finely chopped
¼ cup cilantro, chopped
2 tablespoons fresh coriander
½ teaspoon ground cumin
Sea salt and freshly ground black pepper to taste

Combine all the ingredients in a bowl and mix. Let the relish stand in the refrigerator for at least 4-6 hours, stir frequently.

Tzatziki

This recipe is extremely low in fat. It is delicious served with the Gyros *(See recipe page 54).*

1 cup low fat plain organic yogurt
1 to 3 garlic cloves
2 teaspoons fresh lemon juice
¼ teaspoon salt
½ medium to large cucumber, peeled

Place all of the ingredients in a food processor and purée. Serve chilled.

Makes 2 cups

Nutrition Facts
(Per Serving)

Calories	24
Fat Calories	4
Total Fat	0.5g
Saturated Fat	0.3g
Cholesterol	2mg
Sodium	21mg
Total Carbs	3.1g
Fiber	0.1g
Protein	1.8g

Did You Know…

- Cucumbers are very low in fat.
- Cucumbers are also 95% water.
- Yogurt is an excellent source of calcium and phosphorus.
- Yogurt is more digestible than milk for people who suffer from lactose intolerance.
- Garlic may alleviate nasal congestion.
- Lemon is an excellent source of vitamin C.

salads

Artichoke and Vegetable Pasta Salad

This is a perfect choice for the vegetarian.

8 ounces multi grain rotini pasta
1 cup zucchini, diced
½ cup red bell pepper, diced
½ cup green bell pepper, diced
1 cup marinated artichokes, drained
¼ cup green olives with pimento, sliced
½ cup feta cheese
¼ cup flat leaf parsley, chopped
½ teaspoon sea salt
⅔ cup prepared reduced fat Italian dressing
1 teaspoon cracked black peppercorns

Fill a pot with 3 quarts of water and a dash of salt, and bring to a boil. Add the pasta and cook for 6 – 8 minutes, until the desired tenderness is achieved. Remove from the heat and drain. Rinse with cool water, and drain. Place the pasta in a large mixing bowl and add the zucchini, red pepper, green pepper, artichokes, olives, cheese, parsley and salt. Toss the salad. Drizzle in the Italian dressing. Toss again, blending all the ingredients. Top off with black cracked peppercorns. Serve chilled.

Serves 8 – 10

Nutrition Facts
(Per Serving)

Calories 361
Fat Calories 123
Total Fat 13.6g
Saturated Fat 2.9g
Cholesterol 21mg
Sodium 204mg
Total Carbs 48.2g
Fiber 7.7g
Protein 11.2g

Did You Know…

- Multi grain pasta is an excellent source of whole grains and fiber.
- This rotini pasta is also rich in protein.
- Zucchini consist of approximately 95 % water, which makes this vegetable low in calories. It is also a great source of vitamins C, A and folate.

Asian Shrimp Salad

Serves 6

Nutrition Facts (Per Serving)	
Calories	344
Fat Calories	184
Total Fat	20.4g
Saturated Fat	1.7g
Cholesterol	170mg
Sodium	324mg
Total Carbs	14.4g
Fiber	5g
Protein	25.5g

Did You Know...

- Shrimp is a good source of iron and phosphorous.
- Jicama is an excellent source of vitamin C.
- Consuming bell peppers may reduce the risk of elevated cholesterol levels.

½ cup canola oil
1½ pounds medium shrimp (split lengthwise)
3 tablespoons oyster sauce
2 tablespoons red wine vinegar
1½ teaspoons Dijon mustard
1 tablespoon fresh ginger, chopped
1 teaspoon garlic, chopped
½ pound snow peas
1 medium jicama, peeled and cut into matchsticks
1 cup red bell pepper, thinly sliced
1 cup yellow bell pepper, thinly sliced
½ red onion, halved and thinly sliced
Salt and cracked ground peppercorns to taste
½ cup cilantro, chopped
Lemon wedges, for serving

In a large nonstick skillet, heat 1 tablespoon of the oil over high heat. Add half of the shrimp and sauté until opaque and just cooked through, about 3 minutes. Transfer to a large plate. Repeat with another 1 tablespoon of oil and the remaining shrimp. Let cool.

To make the dressing: In a food processor, combine the oyster sauce with the vinegar, mustard, ginger and garlic, and purée. With the food processor on, gradually add the remaining 6 tablespoons of canola oil.

Bring a medium saucepan of salted water to a boil. Add the snow peas and cook until bright green, about 1½ minutes. Drain the snow peas, refresh under cold water and pat dry. In a serving bowl, combine the snow peas, jicama, peppers, onion and shrimp. Add the dressing, toss well and season with salt and pepper to taste. Sprinkle on the cilantro and serve with lemon wedges.

Authentic Greek Salad

Serves 6

1 pound tomatoes, quartered
1 large cucumber, sliced
½ medium red onion, sliced
1 medium green pepper, sliced
2 tablespoons oregano
¼ cup olive oil
Sea salt and cracked black pepper to taste
1 block fresh feta cheese, served whole

Cut the tomatoes into quarters and place in a large mixing bowl. Slice the cucumber into thin round pieces and add to the tomatoes. Slice the red onion and green pepper into rings, and place them in the bowl. Add the oregano, olive oil, and salt and pepper; mix gently. Place the block of feta cheese on top of the salad and chill. When serving the salad, remove the desired amount of cheese from the block. (One tablespoon of cheese is recommended per serving).

Nutrition Facts
(Per Serving)

Calories	127
Fat Calories	87
Total Fat	9.7g
Saturated Fat	1.4g
Cholesterol	1mg
Sodium	25mg
Total Carbs	8.5g
Fiber	2.1g
Protein	1.3g

Did You Know…

- Red tomatoes have four times the amount of beta carotene as do green tomatoes. Red tomatoes have been proven to help protect against breast, lung, colon, prostate and skin cancers due to the red carotene.
- Cucumbers are an excellent source of silica, a trace mineral that contributes to the strength of connective tissues, such as ligaments.
- Cucumbers contain two compounds---ascorbic acid and caffeic acid---that may help prevent water retention. This is why cucumbers are often used topically for swelling around the eyes.

Broccoli and Cauliflower Salad

Serves 8

Nutrition Facts (Per Serving)	
Calories	115
Fat Calories	62
Total Fat	6.9g
Saturated Fat	0.8g
Cholesterol	8mg
Sodium	496mg
Total Carbs	11.1g
Fiber	2.2g
Protein	2.1g

Did You Know...

- Broccoli is a rich source of lutein which may have anticancer effects.
- Cauliflower is a rich source of vitamin K and vitamin C.
- Carrots promote good night vision.

4 cups broccoli florets
2 cups cauliflower florets
½ cup white onion, diced
¼ cup shredded carrots
1 teaspoon salt
¾ cup reduced fat mayonnaise
¼ cup Splenda
2 tablespoons apple cider vinegar
¼ cup toasted slivered almonds

Place the broccoli, cauliflower, onion, carrots and salt in a mixing bowl. Mix together. In a seperate bowl combine the mayonnaise, Splenda and vinegar, and pour over the broccoli mixture. Refrigerate overnight. Remove and top with the almonds. Serve chilled.

Caesar Salad

This is a light but flavorful dressing I'm sure you will enjoy.

Dressing

¼ to ½ cup extra virgin olive oil
¼ teaspoon dry mustard
2 - 3 dashes Worcestershire sauce
1 teaspoon lemon juice
3 - 4 garlic cloves, minced
1 bunch green onions, white ends only, chopped
Pinch of salt and pepper to taste

Salad

1 large head romaine lettuce, (torn into bite size pieces)
½ bag of Marzetti's Caesar croutons
½ cup shredded Pecorino Romano cheese

In a small bowl, combine the olive oil, dry mustard, Worcestershire sauce and lemon juice. Add the garlic and green onions to the dressing and stir. Salt and pepper to taste. Pour the dressing over the lettuce. Add the croutons and cheese to taste. Finally, toss all of the ingredients together and serve immediately.

Serves 6-8

Nutrition Facts
(Per Serving)

Calories	195
Fat Calories	143
Total Fat	15.9g
Saturated Fat	3.7g
Cholesterol	12mg
Sodium	196mg
Total Carbs	7g
Fiber	1.8g
Protein	5.9g

Did You Know…

- Olive oil helps reduce blood cholesterol levels. It may reduce the risk of heart disease and cancer.
- Garlic helps reduce blood cholesterol levels and also reduces the risk of cancer.
- Garlic is an immune booster.
- Lemons are an excellent source of vitamin C and may also prevent kidney stones.
- Romaine is a good source of chlorophyll and vitamin K. It is also an excellent source of the minerals manganese and chromium.

Chicken Salad

Makes 2 cups

Nutrition Facts (Per Serving)	
Calories	246
Fat Calories	99
Total Fat	11g
Saturated Fat	1.2g
Cholesterol	69mg
Sodium	161mg
Total Carbs	7.7g
Fiber	1g
Protein	29.1g

Did You Know…

- Dark meat chicken contains more fat than white meat chicken.
- Celery is a great source of potassium.
- Walnuts are rich in Omega 3 fatty acids and are a good source of protein.
- Grapes contain phytochemicals that may help guard against heart disease, strokes, and cancer.

1 pound boneless chicken breasts
3½ tablespoons reduced fat mayonnaise
1 tablespoon fresh lemon juice
⅓ cup celery, chopped
⅓ cup walnuts, chopped
⅓ cup green grapes, halved
1 teaspoon white pepper
2 teaspoons Splenda
Pinch of salt

Rinse the chicken breasts and place in a sauce pan with 5 cups of water. Cook on medium heat on a stove top for 35 minutes. Drain the chicken and let cool. Once the chicken has cooled, place it on a cutting board and shred. Place the chicken in a large bowl and stir in the mayonnaise and lemon juice. Add the celery, walnuts, grapes, white pepper, Splenda and salt. Mix thoroughly. Serve chilled.

Egg Salad

Makes 2 cups

6 eggs
2½ tablespoons reduced fat mayonnaise
2 teaspoons Splenda
½ teaspoon yellow mustard

Boil eggs with a pinch of salt for 20 minutes. The salt will ensure the eggs are easier to peel. Drain the eggs and let them cool for 30 minutes. Crack the eggs and remove the outer shell. Cut the eggs in half and discard three whole yolks. Chop the egg whites and remaining yolks. Place the eggs in a bowl and thoroughly blend in the mayonnaise, Splenda, and mustard. Serve chilled.

Nutrition Facts
(Per Serving)

Calories	78
Fat Calories	42
Total Fat	4.7g
Saturated Fat	1.2g
Cholesterol	159mg
Sodium	107mg
Total Carbs	2.4g
Fiber	0g
Protein	6.8g

Did You Know...

- Eggs are a complete protein food.
- Vitamin B12 is found only in animal products such as eggs.
- Eggs are a good source of antioxidants.

Garbanzo Bean Salad

Serves 4

Nutrition Facts (Per Serving)	
Calories	159
Fat Calories	71
Total Fat	7.8g
Saturated Fat	1g
Cholesterol	0g
Sodium	184mg
Total Carbs	17.9g
Fiber	3.7g
Protein	4.2g

This is a light and airy dish that is perfect for the vegan diet.

1 8oz can garbanzo beans, drained
¼ cup red pepper, diced
¼ cup yellow pepper, diced
¼ cup orange pepper, diced
1 cup sugar snap peas, whole
1 tablespoon ground cumin
2 tablespoons olive oil
1 tablespoon fresh lemon juice
Pinch of sea salt
Cracked black peppercorns to taste

Drain the garbanzo beans and set aside in a large bowl. Place the diced peppers in the bowl with the beans. Add the sugar snap peas, cumin, olive oil, lemon juice, salt and pepper to the bowl and toss. Serve immediately.

Did You Know…

- Garbanzo beans are a great source of molybdenum. Molybdenum is a trace mineral that is valuable in assisting the detoxification of sulfites. Sulfites are found in lunch meats and wine.
- Cumin has been touted to aid the digestive system and assist in nutrient assimilation.
- Peas are a good source of protein, phosphorous, magnesium, manganese, potassium and iron.

Grilled Chicken and Raspberry Salad

¼ cup raspberry vinegar
3 tablespoons canola oil
½ teaspoon poppy seeds
¼ teaspoon Splenda
¼ teaspoon salt
¼ teaspoon black pepper
1 pound skinless, boneless chicken breast
6 cups torn Boston lettuce
½ small red onion, thinly sliced and separated into rings
¾ cup raspberries
⅓ cup feta cheese
¼ cup slivered almonds

To prepare the dressing: Combine the raspberry vinegar, canola oil, poppy seeds, Splenda, salt, and pepper. Whisk the ingredients together. Set aside and chill. Preheat the grill to medium heat. Place the chicken on the grill and cook for 18 - 20 minutes, turning once or until fully cooked. Remove from the heat and slice the chicken diagonally.

Line six plates with lettuce. Arrange the chicken on top of the lettuce and top with the red onion rings. Drizzle the dressing and sprinkle with raspberries, feta and almonds.

Serves 6

Nutrition Facts
(Per Serving)

Calories 212
Fat Calories 108
Total Fat 11.9g
Saturated Fat 2.2g
Cholesterol 51mg
Sodium 244mg
Total Carbs 5.6g
Fiber 2.3g
Protein 20.5g

Did You Know…

- Consuming raspberries may reduce the risk of cancer due to their content of ellagic acid. Ellagic acid has been known to block cancer causing air pollutants such as cigarette smoke.
- Raspberries are rich in manganese, fiber and vitamin C.
- Almonds are a great source of Omega 3 fatty acids.

Jules' Potato Salad

Serves 6 to 8

Nutrition Facts (Per Serving)	
Calories	160
Fat Calories	61
Total Fat	6.8g
Saturated Fat	1.8g
Cholesterol	0mg
Sodium	324mg
Total Carbs	22.4g
Fiber	2g
Protein	2.3g

Did You Know...

- Fiber and protein are found in the skin of potatoes.
- Potatoes are rich in potassium, niacin, vitamins B and C, and pantothenic acid.
- Celery contains phytochemical compounds known as coumarins. Coumarins may be useful In lowering blood pressure. Celery is also a rich source of potassium.
- Dill may be useful in promoting detoxification of the liver.

1½ pounds small red potatoes
1 medium celery stalk, chopped
¼ cup shallots, minced
2 tablespoons fresh dill
½ cup reduced fat mayonnaise
½ cup reduced fat sour cream
3 tablespoons fresh lemon juice
Salt and pepper to taste
¼ teaspoon paprika
2 tablespoons fresh parsley

Cut the potatoes into bite size cubes. In a large pot, boil the potatoes in salted water. Drain and let cool. Place the potatoes in a mixing bowl and add the celery, shallots and dill. Mix in the mayonnaise, sour cream and lemon juice. Thoroughly blend all the ingredients. Add salt and pepper. Sprinkle the top of the potato salad with paprika and parsley for garnish. Keep refrigerated until ready to serve.

London Broil and Blue Cheese Salad

Serves 6 to 8

Vinaigrette Dressing and Marinade

3 tablespoons balsamic vinegar
1 tablespoon red wine vinegar
3 tablespoons extra virgin olive oil
1 teaspoon garlic, minced
1 teaspoon shallots, minced
1 teaspoon rosemary, chopped
½ teaspoon sea salt
1 teaspoon cracked black peppercorns

One 16-ounce London Broil
½ red onion, sliced into rings
6 cups torn mixed salad greens
1 cup cherry tomatoes, halved
3 tablespoons crumbled blue cheese
1 cup prepared rye or mixed croutons

To prepare vinaigrette: Combine the balsamic vinegar, red wine vinegar, oil, garlic, shallots, rosemary, salt and pepper. Whisk together and cover. To prepare the marinade (if desired): Double the ingredients for the dressing, reserving half. Place the London Broil in a zip-lock bag and pour in the marinade. Shake well. Marinate for 4 - 6 hours.

Preheat grill on low to medium heat. Place the steak on the grill and cook for 9 – 12 minutes on each side or until the desired temperature is achieved. Grill onions away from flame for 8 minutes or until tender.

Divide the mixed salad greens among four dinner plates. Slice the steak across the grain. Separate the onion slices. Arrange the steak slices and onion rings on top of the greens. Drizzle with reserved vinaigrette. Top with tomatoes, cheese and croutons.

Nutrition Facts
(Per Serving)

Calories	385
Fat Calories	219
Total Fat	24.4g
Saturated Fat	7.6g
Cholesterol	75mg
Sodium	690mg
Total Carbs	13.2g
Fiber	1.5g
Protein	28.3g

Did You Know...

- Beef is a great source of protein.
- Beef is rich in vitamins B12 and B6, both necessary for cellular function.
- It is advised to avoid cooking beef at high temperatures.

Low Fat Coleslaw

Serves 6 - 8

Nutrition Facts (Per Serving)
Calories 84
Fat Calories 55
Total Fat 6.1g
Saturated Fat 0.7g
Cholesterol 7mg
Sodium 275mg
Total Carbs 6.1g
Fiber 1.8g
Protein 1g

Did You Know…

- Cabbage is an excellent source of vitamin C.
- Low in calories and high in fiber.
- May help to protect against colon cancer.

½ small bag shredded cabbage and carrots
½ cup low fat mayonnaise
2 tablespoon apple cider vinegar
2 tablespoons Splenda
1 teaspoon Dijon mustard
1 teaspoon celery seed
¼ teaspoon salt
¼ teaspoon white pepper

Combine all the ingredients in a large bowl. Toss and refrigerate until ready to serve.

Roma Tomato Salad

Serves 4-6

6 Roma tomatoes, diced
1 large cucumber, sliced
½ medium purple onion, sliced
2 ounces fresh mozzarella, diced
1 tablespoon fresh basil, minced
1 teaspoon garlic, minced
Salt and pepper to taste
¼ cup olive oil
¼ cup balsamic vinegar

Dice the tomatoes and place in a large bowl. Slice the cucumber and purple onion and add to the tomatoes. Then, add the mozzarella. Mix in the basil, garlic, salt and pepper. Refrigerate the salad until ready to serve. Finally, pour the oil and vinegar over the salad and toss. Serve immediately.

Nutrition Facts (Per Serving)	
Calories	134
Fat Calories	103
Total Fat	11.5g
Saturated Fat	2.7g
Cholesterol	8mg
Sodium	43mg
Total Carbs	5g
Fiber	0.8g
Protein	2.7g

Did You Know…

- Due to lycopene, an antioxidant, tomatoes may help fight certain cancers.
- Tomatoes are a great source of vitamin C, beta carotene, folate, and potassium.
- Cucumbers are very low in fat.
- Cucumbers are 95% water.
- Onions may help lower blood cholesterol and blood pressure. They also have an antibacterial effect.

Shrimp and Avocado Salad

Serves 8

Nutrition Facts (Per Serving)	
Calories	549
Fat Calories	330
Total Fat	36.6g
Saturated Fat	5.3g
Cholesterol	255mg
Sodium	600mg
Total Carbs	16.1g
Fiber	7.5g
Protein	38.7g

Did You Know…

- Spinach is a rich source of vitamins A and K, folate and potassium.
- Avocados are a rich source of folate, vitamin A and potassium. They are actually a fruit that contains more protein than any other fruit. They are also high in monounsaturated oil.
- Shrimp contains some niacin, vitamin B6 and folate.

3 pounds medium or large shrimp, peeled and deveined
8 small avocados, halved and pitted
2 medium red bell peppers, chopped
2 shallots, finely chopped
¼ cup fresh lemon juice
¼ cup white wine vinegar
½ cup cilantro, chopped
2 garlic cloves, minced
1 teaspoon sea salt
½ teaspoon pepper
½ cup extra virgin olive oil
Baby spinach leaves and lemon wedges, for serving

Bring a large pot of salted water to a boil over medium-high heat. Add the shrimp and simmer until opaque, 3 - 5 minutes. Drain and rinse under cold running water. Transfer to a large bowl. Scoop avocado from the shells and coarsely chop; reserve shells. Add avocado, bell peppers, and shallots to shrimp; mix gently. Whisk together the lemon juice, vinegar, cilantro, garlic, salt, and pepper in a small bowl. Drizzle in olive oil, whisking constantly. Pour the mixture over the shrimp-avocado mixture and mix gently to combine. Line plates with spinach leaves. Place 2 avocado shells on each plate; spoon salad mixture into shells. Serve with lemon wedges.

Soba Noodle and Snow Pea Salad

Serves 4 - 6

- 1/4 cup rice vinegar
- 3 tablespoons reduced-sodium soy sauce
- 1 tablespoon toasted sesame oil
- 1/2 teaspoon Splenda
- 1/2 teaspoon ginger
- 3 cups cooked soba noodles
- 1/2 cup red pepper, cored, seeded and thinly sliced
- 1/2 cup green pepper, cored, seeded and thinly sliced
- 1 cup frozen corn, thawed
- 3/4 cup fresh or frozen snow peas, thawed
- 5 medium scallions, green part only, sliced
- 1/4 cup packed fresh cilantro leaves, chopped

For the dressing: whisk together the vinegar, soy sauce Splenda and ginger. Slowly add the sesame oil. Set aside.

Toss the noodles, peppers, corn, snow peas, scallions and cilantro in a large bowl. Pour in the vinegar dressing. (If it has separated, whisk again before adding). Toss well and serve at once, or cover and chill in the refrigerator up to 24 hours.

Nutrition Facts
(Per Serving)

Calories	232
Fat Calories	20
Total Fat	2.2g
Saturated Fat	0.2g
Cholesterol	0mg
Sodium	1144mg
Total Carbs	43.1g
Fiber	2.6g
Protein	10g

Did You Know...

- Soba noodles contain buckwheat flour that is rich in the flavonoids rutin and quercitin. These flavonoids may help to maintain blood flow in the body.
- Buckwheat may help to reduce blood cholesterol levels.
- Soba noodles are high in protein.

Sweet Broccoli Salad

Serves 6

Nutrition Facts (Per Serving)	
Calories	167
Fat Calories	122
Total Fat	13.6g
Saturated Fat	1.9g
Cholesterol	6mg
Sodium	91mg
Total Carbs	6.4g
Fiber	2.8mg
Protein	4.8g

Did You Know…

- Broccoli is an excellent source of vitamin C, beta carotene and folate.
- Broccoli is rich in glucosinolates that are effective cancer fighters. It is also low in calories and high in fiber.
- Tomatoes have been touted for protection against heart disease. The jelly substance found in tomatoes is high in salicylates which have an anti-clogging effect on the blood.
- Nuts are a good source of protein.

1 large bunch of broccoli, florets only
¼ red onion, sliced
1 cup grape tomatoes, whole
¼ cup pine nuts
¼ cup feta cheese
¼ cup canola oil
2 tablespoons balsamic vinegar
Pinch of Splenda
Cracked black pepper to taste

Chop the broccoli, reserving the florets and place in a large bowl. Add the red onion, grape tomatoes, pine nuts, feta cheese, canola oil, balsamic vinegar, Splenda, and pepper; mix together in bowl. Chill and serve.

Tuna Salad

Serves 2

7 ounces albacore tuna, drained
1½ tablespoons reduced fat mayonnaise
⅓ cup red bell pepper, diced
1 teaspoon fresh lemon juice
1 teaspoon capers, drained
Pinch of white pepper

In a mixing bowl, thoroughly blend the tuna, mayonnaise, red pepper, lemon juice, capers and pepper. Serve chilled.

Nutrition Facts (Per Serving)	
Calories	162
Fat Calories	57
Total Fat	6.3g
Saturated Fat	1.2g
Cholesterol	46mg
Sodium	182mg
Total Carbs	2.6g
Fiber	0.6g
Protein	23.7g

Did You Know…

- Eating two servings of fish per week may reduce the risk of cardiovascular disease.
- Tuna is an excellent source of protein.
- Red peppers are low in calories.

soups & stews

15 Bean Soup

Serves 10

Nutrition Facts (Per Serving)	
Calories	53
Fat Calories	24
Total Fat	2.7g
Saturated Fat	0.4g
Cholesterol	0mg
Sodium	730mg
Total Carbs	6g
Fiber	1.8g
Protein	1.3g

1 pound bag 15 beans
2 bay leaves
1 teaspoon cumin
2 garlic cloves, minced
2 tablespoons olive oil
1 tablespoon salt
Cracked black pepper to taste
1 onion, chopped
2 large celery stalks, chopped
8 ounces carrots, sliced

Soak the beans in water for a minimum of 8 hours. Tie up the bay leaves in a cheesecloth bag. Drain the beans and place them in a large sauce pan with water covering the beans. Add the bay leaves, cumin, garlic, olive oil, and salt and pepper and cook on low to medium heat for 2 hours. Add the onion, celery and carrots. Simmer for an additional ½ hour. Serve warm.

Did You Know…

- Beans contain cholesterol lowering fiber.
- Beans are an excellent source of complex carbohydrates and are very low in fat. They are also a great source of molybdenum and folic acid.
- Beans have been associated with reducing the risk of developing breast cancer.

Autumn Vegetable Stew

Serves 4-6

Nutrition Facts (Per Serving)
Calories 282
Fat Calories 59
Total Fat 6.6g
Saturated Fat 1g
Cholesterol 1mg
Sodium 779mg
Total Carbs 48.6g
Fiber 6.2g
Protein 7.3g

Did You Know...

- Butternut squash is a good source of pantothenic acid, folic acid, vitamin B1 and vitamin C.
- Squash is also a good source of dietary fiber.
- Potatoes contain lysine an essential amino acid.

1 small butternut squash, about 1½ pounds
1 pound red potatoes, unpeeled
1 cup green beans
1 red bell pepper, diced
2 tablespoons olive oil
1 large yellow onion, thinly sliced
1 tablespoon garlic, minced
2 cups low sodium vegetable broth
1½ cups tomatoes, peeled, seeded and chopped
1½ cups corn kernels
1 teaspoon dried sage
1 teaspoon freshly ground pepper

Using a vegetable peeler, peel the squash. Halve it lengthwise, scrape out the seeds and cut into 1" cubes. Cut the potatoes into quarters. Halve the pepper and discard the ribs and seeds. Cut the pepper into 1" squares. Set the vegetables aside.

Warm the oil in a large saucepan over medium heat. Then, add the onion and garlic, and cook, stirring occasionally, until the onion has wilted, about 5 minutes. Add the squash, potatoes, green beans, broth, tomatoes, corn, sage, salt, and pepper, and stir to combine. Bring to a boil over medium high heat. Reduce the heat to low. Cover and simmer for 10 minutes to partially cook the potatoes and squash.

Stir in the bell pepper. Raise the heat to medium and return to a boil. Cover and reduce the heat to low. Simmer until the vegetables are tender, about 15 minutes longer. Serve warm.

Easy Tortellini Soup

One 9-ounce package three cheese tortellini
2 cups organic chicken broth
¼ cup Parmesan cheese
1 tablespoon fresh chives, chopped
1 teaspoon pepper

Place the tortellini in a saucepan with the chicken broth. Gradually bring to a boil and cook 6 - 9 minutes or until the tortellini floats to the top. Remove from heat and place in a serving dish. Some of the chicken broth will evaporate while boiling. Sprinkle on the Parmesan cheese, chives and pepper to taste. Serve warm.

2 servings

Nutrition Facts (Per Serving)	
Calories	232
Fat Calories	72
Total Fat	7.9g
Saturated Fat	4.2g
Cholesterol	30mg
Sodium	758mg
Total Carbs	26.7g
Fiber	1.9g
Protein	13.4g

Did You Know…

- Cheese has fair amounts of protein.
- Organic chicken broth will provide great flavor and is a healthier option than regular canned broth.
- Chicken broth may help relieve cold and flu symptoms.

Five Alarm Turkey Chili

Serves 10

Nutrition Facts
(Per Serving)

Calories	238
Fat Calories	86
Total Fat	9.4g
Saturated Fat	1.8g
Cholesterol	54mg
Sodium	425mg
Total Carbs	20.1g
Fiber	6.6g
Protein	17.8g

Did You Know...

- Turkey is an excellent source of protein.
- Tomatoes are a good source of vitamin C, beta carotene, folate and potassium.
- Beans contain folate and vitamins A and C.
- Cayenne pepper and chili powder have thermogenic properties that may increase metabolism.
- Onions are a good source of vitamin C and beta carotene.

This is a great recipe to prepare in a crock pot. It also freezes well, so you can make it in advance and freeze in individual portions. Then, just pop it in the microwave and in a few minutes you have dinner!

1½ pounds ground turkey
Lawry's seasoned salt and pepper
29 ounces canned stewed tomatoes
15 ounces canned black beans, drained
½ large onion, minced
4 cups water
2 tablespoons canola oil
2 tablespoons chili powder
2 teaspoons dried red pepper flakes
1 tablespoon salt
2 teaspoons ground cumin
1 teaspoon dried oregano
1 teaspoon cayenne pepper
1 tablespoon Splenda
2 tablespoons paprika
2 tablespoons wheat flour

Slightly brown the turkey in a large skillet. Season the turkey with Lawry's seasoned salt and pepper to taste. Drain the excess liquid from the turkey, then place the turkey in a large stock pot or crock pot. Add the stewed tomatoes, black beans, and onion. Then, add the water, canola oil, chili powder, red pepper flakes, salt, cumin, oregano, cayenne pepper, Splenda, paprika and flour. Let simmer for 4- 6 hours in a crock pot.

Tortilla Chicken Soup

Serves 8
(1 cup servings)

Nutrition Facts (Per Serving)	
Calories	208
Fat Calories	43
Total fat	4.7g
Saturated Fat	0.9g
Cholesterol	48mg
Sodium	511mg
Total Carbs	17.8g
Fiber	5.9g
Protein	23.4g

1 cup onion, chopped
2 teaspoons garlic, minced
1 tablespoon olive oil
4 cups organic chicken broth
2 cups water
One 15 ounce can diced tomatoes
One 4 ounce can diced green chilies
One 15 ounce can black beans, drained and rinsed
1½ tablespoons chili powder
1½ tablespoons cumin
1 teaspoon cracked black pepper
3 cups cooked, diced chicken breast
¼ cup lime juice
3 tablespoons fresh cilantro, chopped

Homemade tortilla chips to garnish
(See recipe page 6)

Prepare tortilla chips and set aside. In a soup pot, heat the olive oil and sauté the onions until golden. Add the garlic and sauté another 1 - 2 minutes. Add all of the remaining ingredients, except the lime juice and cilantro, and simmer 25- 30 minutes. Stir in the lime juice and cilantro. Add chips to garnish. Serve warm.

Did You Know...

- Beans contain folate and vitamins A and C.
- Beans are high in protein and iron.
- Tomatoes are a useful source of potassium.
- Green chilies are an excellent source of beta carotene and vitamin C. They are also rich in bioflavonoids which may prevent cancer.

White Chicken Chili

Serves 10

Nutrition Facts (Per Serving)	
Calories	305
Fat Calories	41
Total Fat	4.5g
Saturated Fat	1.2g
Cholesterol	55mg
Sodium	600mg
Total Carbs	33.6g
Fiber	10.2g
Protein	32.4g

Did You Know...

- Beans provide an excellent source of complex carbohydrates and fiber.
- Beans may help reduce cholesterol.
- Chicken is low in fat.

Note this dish is delicious served with Fiesta Cornbread (See recipe page 85)

1 pound Great Northern beans
6 cups organic chicken broth
1 tablespoon canola oil
3 garlic cloves, minced
1½ cups onions, chopped
8 ounces green chilies, chopped
2 tablespoons jalapeño peppers, minced
2 teaspoons cumin
1 teaspoon oregano
¼ teaspoon cloves, ground
5 cups boneless chicken breasts, cubed
1 teaspoon white pepper
½ teaspoon salt
½ cup Tomatillo Salsa (See recipe page 15)
⅓ cup reduced fat sour cream

Combine the beans, broth, oil, garlic, onion, green chilies, jalapeños, cumin, oregano, cloves, chicken, pepper and salt in a crock pot. Cook on medium heat for 2½ to 3 hours, or until the beans are tender. Stir frequently. Remove from the heat and place in serving bowls. Top off with a splash of tomatillo salsa and a teaspoon of sour cream.

meat

Barbecue Chicken

2 pounds chicken breasts, bone in
1 teaspoon seasoned salt
Barbecue Sauce (see recipe below)

Barbecue Sauce

Yields 1¼ cups

1 cup ketchup
½ cup water
⅓ cup white vinegar
2 tablespoons Worcestershire sauce
¼ cup Splenda brown sugar
1 tablespoon dried onion
1 teaspoon cayenne pepper
¼ teaspoon salt

For the Barbecue Sauce: Mix together all the ingredients and set aside.

Preheat the grill to medium. Rinse the chicken breasts and remove the skin. Season the chicken breasts with seasoned salt, and place directly on the grill. Depending on the size of the breasts, grill for approximately 20 minutes, turning frequently. Brush on the Barbecue Sauce and cook for an additional 5 minutes or until the juices run clear.

Serves 6

Nutrition Facts
(Per Serving)

Calories	327
Fat Calories	51
Total Fat	5.6g
Saturated Fat	1.5g
Cholesterol	130mg
Sodium	248mg
Total Carbs	21.5g
Fiber	1g
Protein	47.7g

Did You Know...

- Consuming chicken in moderate amounts supports digestive function.
- Free- range organically fed chickens are now available in most supermarkets.
- White chicken meat is a low fat source of protein.

BLT

Serves 6

Nutrition Facts (Per Serving)	
Calories	390
Fat Calories	134
Total Fat	14.9g
Saturated Fat	4g
Cholesterol	65mg
Sodium	1372mg
Total Carbs	45.7g
Fiber	7.7g
Protein	19.9g

Did You Know...

- Turkey bacon is a healthier alternative to pork bacon because it contains far less fat.
- Spinach contains adequate amounts of vitamins C, B6 and riboflavin.
- Tomatoes are rich in antioxidants. Antioxidants provide protection against negative free radicals that damage our cells.

1 pound turkey bacon
6 whole wheat bagels, sliced
⅓ cup roasted red pepper hummus, divided (See recipe page 7)
1 cup fresh spinach, whole leaf without stalks
1 tomato, sliced

Cook the turkey bacon in a skillet on low heat for 20 minutes, or until brown. Lightly toast the bagels in a toaster oven for 5 minutes or in a toaster. Spread a tablespoon of hummus on half of each bagel. Layer the spinach and tomato on top of the hummus. Remove the bacon from the skillet and place on a paper towel to absorb excess fat. Once the bacon has cooled slightly, place on sandwiches and serve warm.

Note: The hummus recipe calls for black olives. You may substitute a ½ cup of roasted red peppers.

Chicken and Cabbage with Sesame Dressing

Serves 4

- ¼ cup Italian salad dressing, prepared
- 1 tablespoon soy sauce
- 1 teaspoon toasted sesame oil
- ¼ teaspoon crushed red pepper
- 2 tablespoons fresh ginger, grated
- 3 cups shredded cabbage with carrots, prepared
- 2½ cups of cooked chicken, sliced
- 1 head Boston lettuce, separated into leaves
- ¼ cup sesame seeds, toasted

For dressing, in a small bowl combine Italian salad dressing, soy sauce, sesame oil, crushed red pepper and ginger. Set aside.

In a large bowl, toss together cabbage mixture, and chicken. Drizzle with dressing; toss gently to coat.

Line 4 dinner plates with lettuce leaves. Sprinkle with sesame seeds.

Nutrition Facts
(Per Serving)

Calories	309
Fat Calories	148
Total Fat	16.5g
Saturated Fat	2.7g
Cholesterol	77mg
Sodium	335mg
Total Carbs	9.8g
Fiber	4.3g
Protein	30.5g

Did You Know…

- Cabbage is low in calories and rich in manganese, magnesium, calcium, biotin, folic acid, vitamin B6, potassium and vitamin C.
- Cabbage may help to alleviate peptic ulcers.
- Ginger may help to soothe the intestinal tract.

Chicken Cacciatore

Serves 6

Nutrition Facts (Per Serving)	
Calories	410
Fat Calories	118
Total Fat	13.2g
Saturated Fat	2.2g
Cholesterol	88mg
Sodium	548mg
Total Carbs	34g
Fiber	6.3g
Protein	38.8g

Did You Know…

- Chicken contains lysine. Lysine promotes the building of muscle protein. It is particularly helpful for those who may be recovering from an injury or a recent surgery.
- Tomatoes are low in calories and provide up to four times the amount of beta carotene as opposed to green tomatoes.
- Mushrooms are an excellent source of a variety of many minerals.

This recipe is great prepared in a crock pot and cooked slowly, allowing all of the flavors to blend together.

2 pounds boneless chicken breasts, cubed
Two 16-ounce cans stewed tomatoes
Two 4-ounce cans tomato paste
1 tablespoon oregano
1 tablespoon basil
1 teaspoon red pepper flakes
4 medium garlic cloves, minced
1 medium green pepper, diced
1 medium red pepper, diced
1 small Spanish onion, diced
1 cup button mushrooms, sliced
⅓ cup olive oil
1 teaspoon Splenda
1 pound whole wheat pasta

Place the chicken cubes and olive oil in the crock pot and turn on low heat. Add the stewed tomatoes, tomato paste, oregano, basil, red pepper flakes, Splenda and garlic cloves; blend thoroughly. Place the green pepper, red pepper, and Spanish onion in the crock pot. Slice the mushrooms and add to the ingredients. Cook on low heat for 4 - 6 hours until ready to serve.

Chicken Quesadillas

Enjoy this dish as a meal or as a snack.

Salsa

1 cup ripe tomatoes, diced, or one 8 ounce can
½ Spanish onion, coarsely chopped
2 - 3 tablespoons fresh cilantro, chopped (optional)
1 - 2 tablespoons fresh lime juice
1 tablespoon jalapeños, diced
1 - 2 tablespoons green chiles, diced
Salt and pepper to taste

Quesadillas

1 pound boneless, skinless chicken breasts (already prepared chicken may be substituted)
¼ teaspoon salt
¼ teaspoon chili powder
¼ teaspoon ground cumin
1 tablespoon olive oil
Four 8" whole wheat tortillas
2 cups Monterey Jack cheese, grated
¼ teaspoon cracked black pepper

For the Salsa: Combine the tomatoes, onion, cilantro, lime juice, jalapeños, green chiles, and salt and pepper in a food processor, and purée.

For the Quesadillas: Halve the chicken breasts lengthwise. Mix the salt, chili powder and cumin in a bowl; sprinkle over the chicken. Heat the oil in a large nonstick skillet over medium heat. Add the chicken and cook until opaque inside, 3 - 4 minutes per side. Transfer to a cutting board and let cool slightly; slice thinly.

Place a tortilla on a quesadilla maker or portable grill. Sprinkle one half of the tortilla with ¼ cup of the cheese; top with ¼ of the sliced chicken. Cook until the cheese begins to melt, about 1 minute. Sprinkle with another ¼ cup of the cheese and the black pepper. Fold the tortilla in half over the chicken. Continue to cook, turning once or twice, until crispy on both sides, 2 - 3 minutes. Transfer to a prepared baking sheet and keep warm in the oven while repeating with the remaining tortillas, cheese and chicken.

Cut the quesadillas into wedges. Serve with salsa and garnish with scallion greens.

Serves 4

Nutrition Facts
(Per Serving)

Calories	420
Fat Calories	176
Total Fat	19.6g
Saturated Fat	9.8g
Cholesterol	104mg
Sodium	629mg
Total Carbs	20.9g
Fiber	1.8g
Protein	40g

Did You Know…

- Chicken is a great source of protein and is rich in vitamin A, the B vitamins and minerals.
- Cumin has potential antioxidant and cancer fighting properties.
- Cheese is a great source of protein and calcium.

Dijon Sirloin and Black Cracked Peppercorn Kebabs

Serves 4

Nutrition Facts (Per Serving)	
Calories	317
Fat Calories	111
Total Fat	12.3g
Saturated Fat	4.2g
Cholesterol	67mg
Sodium	363mg
Total Carbs	17.6g
Fiber	5.1g
Protein	22.9g

Did You Know…

- Beef is a great source of high quality protein.
- Beef contains a wide range of nutrients, such as vitamin B12, iron, niacin, and zinc.
- Peppers are an excellent low calorie source of beta carotene and vitamin C.
- Mushrooms are fat free and very low in calories.
- This marinade is virtually fat free.

1 pound sirloin steak, cubed
8 ounces mushrooms, whole
1 large Spanish onion, quartered
2 large green bell peppers, cubed
2 large red bell peppers, cubed
8 ounces cherry tomatoes, whole

Marinade

½ cup Dijon mustard
¼ cup cracked black peppercorns
½ cup Worcestershire sauce

For the marinade: Cube the sirloin steak in advance and place in a zip lock plastic bag. In a measuring cup, whisk together the Dijon mustard, black peppercorns and Worcestershire sauce. Pour the marinade over the steak and refrigerate a minimum of 6 hours for the best flavor.

If using wooden skewers, soak them in water for about half an hour so they don't burn. Cut the onion, green and red peppers into medium sized cubes. Leave the mushrooms and tomatoes whole. Skewer all the vegetables and steak in colorful layers for presentation purposes. Place on the grill and cook on low to medium heat. Do not overcook.

Suggestion: Serve over a bed of brown rice that has been prepared in beef broth instead of water. Or, simply serve over long grain and wild rice.

Enchiladas

Serves 6

- 1 tablespoon canola oil
- 1 pound ground turkey
- ½ Spanish onion, chopped
- One 10-ounce can chopped tomatoes
- One 4-ounce can diced green chilies
- 1 garlic clove, minced
- 2 tablespoons flaked red pepper
- 2 tablespoons ground cumin
- 2 tablespoons chili powder
- 1 tablespoon paprika
- 1 teaspoon black pepper
- 5 whole wheat tortillas
- ½ cup sharp cheddar cheese, shredded
- ½ cup salsa (See recipe 12)
- ⅓ cup reduced fat sour cream
- One 4-ounce can black olives, sliced and drained

Preheat the oven to 350°. Add the canola oil to a skillet and bring to medium heat. Add the ground turkey and lightly brown on medium heat for 5 minutes. Add the onion, tomatoes, green chilies, and garlic; simmer on low heat. Blend in the red pepper flakes, cumin, chili powder, paprika and black pepper. Simmer on low heat for 15 minutes or until the liquid has evaporated; remove from the skillet. Coat a 9" x 11" baking dish with cooking spray. Place the tortillas in the baking dish and fill with the turkey mixture. Roll the tortillas, sealing in the ingredients. Repeat with the remaining tortillas. Bake for 20 minutes. Remove from the oven and sprinkle on a light layer of cheese and bake for an additional 10 minutes. Remove from the oven and serve warm. Top with the salsa, sour cream and black olives.

Nutrition Facts
(Per Serving)

Calories	258
Fat Calories	107
Total Fat	11.9g
Saturated Fat	3.5g
Cholesterol	51mg
Sodium	557mg
Total Carbs	21.7g
Fiber	3.6g
Protein	16.1g

Did You Know…

- Turkey has high levels of the amino acid tryptophan. Tryptophan is a necessary component of serotonin which helps to induce sleep.
- A 3.5 oz serving of turkey contains 2,450 mg of Lysine. Lysine has been touted for the treatment of Herpes Simplex.
- Lycopene, which is abundantly found in tomatoes, may provide valuable protection against prostate cancer.

Grilled Turkey Kielbasa

Serves 6

Nutrition Facts (Per Serving)	
Calories	400
Fat Calories	161
Total Fat	18g
Saturated Fat	3.5g
Cholesterol	49mg
Sodium	1049mg
Total Carbs	42.1g
Fiber	5.6g
Protein	17.7g

Did You Know...

- Turkey is a healthier alternative to beef or pork sausage.
- One medium green pepper contains 100 percent of the Recommended Dietary Allowance for vitamin C.
- Onions contain sulfur compounds that have been shown to block carcinogens.

1 pound turkey smoked sausage
1 large onion, sliced
2 medium green bell peppers, sliced
⅓ cup olive oil
4 teaspoons prepared spicy honey mustard
6 slices whole wheat bread

Preheat grill on low heat. Place sausage away from the flame and cook for 25 minutes, turning once. Be sure to close the grill and trap the heat. In a large bowl, toss the onion and green pepper in the olive oil. Place the vegetables in a grill basket and grill for 15 minutes on medium to low heat or until tender. To avoid burning the vegetables, keep them away from direct flame. Remove from grill. Spread the mustard on the bread and place the turkey and vegetables inside the bread. Serve warm.

Gyros

A perfect accompaniment to the gyros is the Tzatziki (See recipe page 18).

- ¼ cup lettuce, shredded
- 2 slices tomato
- 2 rings green bell pepper
- ½ whole wheat pita pocket
- 4 ounces prepared chicken or lamb (marinated), sliced
- ¼ cupTzatziki sauce (see pg.19)
- 1 tablespoon black olives, diced

Cut vegetables and set aside. Lightly toast the pita pocket and fill with lettuce, tomato, and green peppers. Add the chicken or lamb and drizzle on Tzatziki sauce. Finish with diced black olives.

Serves 1

Nutrition Facts
(Per Serving)

Calories	299
Fat Calories	53
Total Fat	5.9g
Saturated Fat	1.3g
Cholesterol	96mg
Sodium	332mg
Total Carbs	22.5g
Fiber	4g
Protein	39.1g

Did You Know…

- Chicken may be helpful for building energy and supporting the digestive system and its functions.
- Whole wheat may provide protection against colon and breast cancers.
- Green peppers are a cholesterol lowering vegetable.

Healthy Pepperoni Pizza

Serves 8 as an appetizer, 2 as an entrée

Nutrition Facts
(One pita pocket per serving)

Calories	368
Fat Calories	100
Total Fat	11.2g
Saturated Fat	4.8g
Cholesterol	40mg
Sodium	1332mg
Total Carbs	45.2g
Fiber	6.8g
Protein	21.2g

Did You Know…

- The pita is considered a Middle Eastern bread.
- Wheat is a good source of fiber, niacin, riboflavin, iron and other B vitamins.
- Onions may lower elevated blood pressure and cholesterol.
- Cheese is high in protein.

This is a quick and easy meal for the entire family.

2 large (sandwich size) whole wheat pita pockets
½ cup prepared tomato sauce
½ cup onion, chopped
¼ cup black olives, minced
10 to 12 slices turkey pepperoni
½ cup reduced fat part-skim mozzarella cheese

Spread the tomato sauce on top of the whole wheat pita pocket. Place the onions, black olives and turkey pepperoni on top of the tomato sauce. Sprinkle the cheese on top. Bake in a toaster oven up to 10 minutes, being careful not to burn the cheese. Serve warm.

Jambalaya

2 tablespoons olive oil, divided
1 cup yellow onion, chopped
1 cup celery, chopped
1 cup green bell pepper, chopped
2 garlic cloves, minced
1½ pounds boneless, skinless chicken breasts, cut into chunks
1 bay leaf
½ cup uncooked brown rice
1 teaspoon fresh thyme, chopped, or ½ teaspoon dried
¼ cup fresh parsley, chopped
One 14½ ounce can diced tomatoes in juice
¾ pound rope link turkey sausage, sliced
1 pound large shrimp, peeled and deveined
½ cup Tabasco (optional)
½ can lite beer

Heat 1 tablespoon of the oil in a large nonstick skillet. Add the onion, celery and bell pepper. Cook, stirring frequently, until softened, about 7 minutes. Add the garlic and cook until vegetables begin to brown and the garlic is quite fragrant, 2 to 3 minutes longer. Transfer to a large crock pot.

Heat the remaining tablespoon of oil in a skillet. Add the chicken and cook until browned, about 3 minutes on each side. Transfer to the crock pot and add the bay leaf, rice, thyme, parsley, tomatoes, hot sauce, beer, and turkey sausage. Cover and cook until the flavors blend and the rice and chicken are tender, 5 hours on Low or 3 hours on High. Ten minutes before the end of the cooking time, gently stir in the shrimp. Cover and cook until the shrimp are pink and opaque, about 10 minutes. Remove bay leaf. Serve warm.

Serves 8
(1½ cup each)

Nutrition Facts	
Calories	346
Fat Calories	103
Total Fat	11.5g
Saturated Fat	2.5g
Cholesterol	171mg
Sodium	879mg
Total Carbs	19.1g
Fiber	2.1g
Protein	41.5g

Did You Know…

- Brown rice is healthy filler to most soups.
- Chicken contains niacin.
- Shrimp is a great source of iron and phosphorous.

Oven Roasted Chicken

Serves 4 - 6

Nutrition Facts (Per Serving)	
Calories	434
Fat Calories	207
Total Fat	23g
Saturated Fat	51g
Cholesterol	169mg
Sodium	167mg
Total Carbs	1.8g
Fiber	0.5g
Protein	55g

Did You Know…

- Chicken is rich in protein, selenium, niacin, and vitamin B6. The breast of the chicken is considerably lower in fat and calories than the other parts of the chicken.
- Discarding the skin will reduce total fat and calories.
- Leftover chicken is great in chicken soup which has been known to help alleviate common cold symptoms.

1 whole chicken
1 large shallot
½ medium celery stalk
2 garlic cloves, whole
¼ cup olive oil
1 teaspoon seasoned salt
1 teaspoon dried oregano
1 teaspoon dried thyme
1 teaspoon paprika
Cracked black pepper to taste

Preheat the oven to 375°. Rinse the chicken and clean out the cavity. Place the chicken, breast side up, on a roasting rack with a shallow roasting pan underneath to collect the drippings. Stuff the cavity of the chicken with the shallot, celery stalk and garlic cloves. Generously brush the skin with olive oil. The oil will create crunchy skin and help the herbs adhere to the skin. Sprinkle the chicken with the seasoned salt, oregano, thyme, paprika, and cracked black pepper. Bake at 375°, uncovered.

Note: *Generally speaking, a 2½ 3 lb. chicken will cook in approximately 1¼ hours. Or, cook until the juices run clear.*

Red Currant Cornish Hens

Serves 2-4

2 whole Cornish Hens
½ orange, quartered
½ Vidalia onion, quartered
2 small garlic cloves, whole
½ cup red currant jelly

Preheat the oven to 350°. Coat a 9" x 11" baking dish with cooking spray. Rinse the Cornish hens and stuff the cavities with ¼ of the orange, ¼ of the onion and one garlic clove. Bake the hens for 35 minutes. Remove from the oven and generously brush the exterior of the hens with red currant jelly. Place back in the oven for an additional 10 minutes. Cool slightly and serve.

Nutrition Facts
(Per Serving)

Calories	401
Fat Calories	212
Total Fat	23.5g
Saturated Fat	6.5g
Cholesterol	168mg
Sodium	92mg
Total Carbs	19g
Fiber	1.9g
Protein	29.5g

Did You Know…

- Poultry is an excellent source of protein.
- Oranges provide an excellent source of vitamin C that bolsters the immune system. They also contain Hesperidin which has been shown to decrease blood pressure and cholesterol. Hesperidin is found in the white pulp of the orange.
- Onions are also known to decrease blood pressure.
- Garlic may provide protection against atherosclerosis.

Sesame Beef and Vegetable Stir-Fry

Serves 6

Nutrition Facts	
Calories	305
Fat calories	77
Total Fat	8.5g
Saturated Fat	1.8g
Cholesterol	45mg
Sodium	686mg
Total Carbs	32.4g
Fiber	7g
Protein	24.6g

Did You Know...

- Lean beef is an excellent source of protein.
- Lean organic beef contains high amounts of vitamin B12.
- Ginger contains properties that may assist in digestive health.

Sauce

1 tablespoon cornstarch
1 cup organic beef broth
3 tablespoons reduced-sodium soy sauce
2 tablespoons dry sherry
½ teaspoon toasted sesame oil
½ teaspoon hot chili oil
½ teaspoon dried red pepper flakes

Beef and Vegetable Mixture

1 teaspoon canola oil, plus 1 teaspoon
1 pound sirloin, well trimmed and cut into thin strips
6 cups broccoli florets
1 bunch scallions, cut diagonally
3 teaspoons garlic, finely chopped
2 tablespoons fresh ginger, minced
1 cup baby corn, drained
½ cup red pepper, chopped
12 ounces whole wheat fettuccine, cooked and drained
Cracked black peppercorns to taste
3 tablespoons sesame seeds

For the Sauce: In a small bowl, whisk the cornstarch with the broth, soy sauce, sherry, sesame oil, chili oil, pepper flakes, and ¼ cup water. Set aside. Toast the sesame seeds in a small skillet over medium heat, stirring occasionally, until fragrant, about 5 minutes. Set aside.

For the Beef and Vegetables: Heat 1 teaspoon of the oil in a wok over high heat. Add the beef and stir-fry it until the meat is seared, 2 or 3 minutes. Remove and set aside. Add the remaining 1 teaspoon of oil to the pan. Add the broccoli, baby corn, red pepper and stir-fry until it is crisp-tender, about 2-3 minutes. Add the scallions and stir-fry for 1 minute. Add the garlic and ginger and stir-fry for 60 seconds. Reduce the heat to medium. Stir the sauce mixture and add it to the pan. Cook, stirring almost constantly, until the sauce comes to a boil, thickens and turns translucent, about 3 minutes. Stir in the beef and juices and heat thoroughly. Season with salt and pepper to taste.

To Serve: Spoon the meat and vegetable mixture over the fettuccine and sprinkle with the sesame seeds.

Spicy Goulash

Serves 4 - 6

- 1 tablespoon olive oil
- 1 pound ground turkey
- ½ cup yellow onion, diced
- 28 ounces stewed tomatoes
- 8 ounces tomato sauce
- 6 ounces tomato paste
- 1 tablespoon garlic, minced
- 1 teaspoon oregano
- 1 teaspoon cayenne pepper
- ¼ teaspoon black pepper
- ½ teaspoon Splenda
- 1 teaspoon basil
- 8 ounces whole wheat macaroni

Place the olive oil, ground turkey and onions in a skillet and lightly brown for 10 minutes. Meanwhile, in a stock pot add the tomatoes, tomato sauce, tomato paste, garlic, oregano, cayenne pepper, black pepper, and Splenda and simmer on low heat. Drain the turkey mixture and add to the stock pot. Cook on medium to low heat for two hours. Add the basil. Place the whole wheat macaroni in a saucepan with 3 quarts of water and a dash of olive oil. Cook for 6 - 8 minutes or until the pasta reaches the desired tenderness. Remove from the heat drain. Add the pasta to sauce. Serve warm.

Nutrition Facts
(Per Serving)

Calories	308
Fat Calories	91
Total Fat	10.1g
Saturated Fat	2.7g
Cholesterol	90mg
Sodium	584mg
Total Carbs	29.6g
Fiber	5.1g
Protein	24.6g

Did You Know…

- Tomatoes may help protect against heart disease, largely due to the content of salicylates which have an anti-clotting effect on the blood.
- Turkey is an excellent source of niacin. Niacin is important for having healthy skin, and healthy nervous and digestive systems.
- Dark meat turkey is high in selenium.

Turkey Meatloaf

Serves 6

Nutrition Facts (Per Serving)	
Calories	296
Fat Calories	100
Total Fat	11.2g
Saturated Fat	2.9g
Cholesterol	101mg
Sodium	418mg
Total Carbs	23.6g
Fiber	3.5g
Protein	25.5g

Did You Know...

- Turkey is an excellent source of high quality protein, with all the essential amino acids, as well as calcium, copper, iron, phosphorus, potassium, and zinc.
- Eggs whites are also an excellent source of lean protein.

This recipe takes a traditional homestyle meatloaf and works a little healthy magic! This is something the entire family can enjoy. It's great as a leftover, may be served hot or cold, and on a sandwich.

1½ pounds lean ground turkey
½ cup onion, finely chopped
4 egg whites, 1 yolk
1 cup salsa, (See recipe 12)
¾ cup oats
1 package vegetable soup mix
¼ teaspoon ground pepper
Salt to taste
½ cup ketchup

Preheat the oven to 350°. In a large mixing bowl, combine the ground turkey, onion, egg whites, yolk, salsa, oats, soup mix, pepper and salt. Place the mixture in a 9" x 5" pan and pour the ketchup on top. Bake for approximately 60 minutes.

Serving suggestions: The Traditional Mashed Potatoes (See recipe 110) are a nice complement for a hearty meal that is high in lean protein and very low in fat.

Veal Parmesan

This is a very rich recipe your family is sure to enjoy.

4 veal cutlets
2 egg whites
1 cup whole wheat seasoned bread crumbs
⅓ cup olive oil
Four servings of whole wheat pasta, cooked
½ cup shredded part-skim mozzarella cheese
Italian tomato gravy (See recipe page 111)
¼ cup Parmesan cheese, grated

Pound the veal cutlets thin with a mallet. Place the eggs whites in a bowl and the spread the bread crumbs evenly on a plate. Dip each cutlet in the egg whites, and then roll each cutlet in the bread crumbs. Heat a large skillet with olive oil on medium heat. Place each cutlet in the skillet and simmer on medium heat for 5 minutes until the bread crumbs have adhered to the veal. Then reduce heat and simmer for an additional 12 - 15 minutes on low heat until the cutlets have browned. Remove from the heat and drain the excess olive oil. Place the veal on a bed of whole wheat pasta and sprinkle with mozzarella cheese. Pour on the Italian tomato gravy. Add the Parmesan cheese to taste.

Serves 4

Nutrition Facts
(Per Serving)

Calories	497
Fat Calories	278
Total Fat	31.2g
Saturated Fat	8.7g
Cholesterol	55mg
Sodium	390mg
Total Carbs	30.3g
Fiber	4.9g
Protein	24.4g

Did You Know...

- Veal is a source of protein.
- Egg whites are also a good source of protein.
- Whole wheat pasta is a good source of complex carbohydrates.

pastas@grains

Garlic and Tomato Wheat Ravioli

Serves 4

1 cup tomatoes, chopped
3 garlic cloves, minced
¼ cup olive oil
¼ cup fresh lemon juice
9 ounces four cheese whole wheat ravioli
⅓ cup fresh basil, snipped
Cracked black peppercorn to taste

Sauté the tomatoes, garlic, olive oil and lemon juice for 8 - 10 minutes. Bring the pasta to a rapid boil for approximately 6 - 9 minutes or until the pasta floats to the top. Drain the pasta and place in a bowl. Add the tomato and garlic sauce and toss. Sprinkle on the basil and black peppercorns. Serve warm.

Nutrition Facts
(Per Serving)

Calories	224
Fat Calories	145
Total Fat	16.1g
Saturated Fat	3.4g
Cholesterol	16mg
Sodium	177mg
Total Carbs	15.1g
Fiber	2g
Protein	4.7g

Did You Know…

- Whole wheat pasta is rated lower on the glycemic index that regular white pasta.
- Cheese is a good source of calcium.
- Garlic has been touted to help alleviate respiratory infections.

Italian Tomato Gravy with Angel Hair Pasta

Serves 6

Nutrition Facts
(Per Serving)

Calories	159
Fat Calories	72
Total fat	8.1g
Saturated Fat	2.3g
Cholesterol	7mg
Sodium	250mg
Total Carbs	15.2g
Fiber	2.5g
Protein	6.3g

Did You Know...

- Tomatoes are a great source of vitamin C, beta carotene, folate, and potassium.
- Tomatoes are also a great source of lycopene, an anti-oxidant that has been known to fight or ward off certain cancers. Lycopene is found in the skin of the tomato. The deeper the color of the tomato, the more nutritionally dense it is.
- Wheat pasta contains three times the amount of fiber as white pasta. It is also rated lower than white pasta on the glycemic index.
- Garlic may help prevent or lower blood pressure and elevated blood cholesterol levels.

2 to 3 tablespoons olive oil
5 large garlic cloves, minced
24 ounces stewed tomatoes
1 small can tomato paste
½ cup dry red wine
1 tablespoon oregano
1 tablespoon basil
1 tablespoon red pepper flakes
¼ cup black olives, minced
½ cup Parmesan cheese, grated
1 pound whole wheat angel hair pasta

Heat the olive oil in a sauce pan and add the garlic. Brown the garlic for approximately two minutes. Add the tomatoes, tomato paste, wine, oregano, basil, red pepper flakes and black olives. Simmer on low heat for 40 - 60 minutes. Cook the pasta 2 - 5 minutes in a large pot of boiling, salted water to which you have added a splash of olive oil. Do not over-cook. Drain and toss with half of the Parmesan cheese. To serve, pour the tomato sauce over a bed of angel hair pasta and top off with the remaining Parmesan cheese.

Spaghetti and Turkey Meatballs

Serves 6

Meatballs

16 ounces ground turkey
⅓ cup seasoned bread crumbs
1 teaspoon dried oregano
1 teaspoon garlic, minced
1 egg
½ teaspoon salt
1 teaspoon pepper

1 pound whole wheat spaghetti
Dash of olive oil
Pinch of salt

Tomato Sauce

28 ounces canned stewed tomatoes
16 ounces tomato sauce
6 ounces tomato paste
⅓ cup onion, diced
1 tablespoons dried oregano
1 tablespoons garlic, minced
½ teaspoon red pepper flakes
1 tablespoon olive oil
½ teaspoon Splenda
½ teaspoon salt
⅓ cup fresh basil, chopped
⅓ cup Parmesan cheese
Black cracked peppercorns to taste

Place the turkey, bread crumbs, oregano, garlic, egg, salt and pepper in a food processor. Blend for two minutes or until the meat mixture becomes tacky. Remove and roll the meat mixture into medium size balls. Place in a large skillet that has been coated with cooking spray and brown for 10 minutes.

For the Tomato Sauce: Place the stewed tomatoes, tomato sauce, tomato paste, onion, oregano, garlic, red pepper flakes, olive oil, Splenda and salt in a large crock pot. Turn the crock pot on low heat. Remove the meatballs from the skillet and place in the crock pot. Stir gently to blend the ingredients and to prevent the meatballs from falling apart. Cook on low heat for 3 hours or until ready to serve.

Boil the whole wheat pasta in water with the olive oil and the salt. Cook for 6 - 9 minutes. Drain the pasta. Pour the meatball sauce over a bed of pasta. Sprinkle on fresh basil, parmesan cheese and peppercorns. Serve warm.

Nutrition Facts
(Per Serving)

Calories	282
Fat Calories	67
Total Fat	7.6g
Saturated Fat	1.7g
Cholesterol	45mg
Sodium	356mg
Total Carbs	36g
Fiber	7g
Protein	17.7g

Did You Know…

- Turkey is an excellent source of low fat, high protein food.
- There is five times more lycopene in tomato paste as there is in raw tomatoes.
- Basil contains two important flavonoids, orientin and vicenin. These water soluble flavonoids have been shown to protect cells from free radical damage.

Whole Wheat Lasagna

Serves 8

Nutrition Facts (Per Serving)	
Calories	298
Fat Calories	135
Total Fat	15.1g
Saturated Fat	6.1g
Cholesterol	65mg
Sodium	544mg
Total Carbs	12.5g
Fiber	1.9g
Protein	28.3g

Did You Know...

- Turkey is a great source of vitamin A, B vitamins and minerals. Turkey contains tryptophan, an essential amino acid that may help ease the symptoms of insomnia and depression.
- Whole grains have proven to lower the risk of diabetes, heart disease and some cancers.
- Spinach contains folate, a nutrient that is important for women who are pregnant or planning to conceive. Folate has been touted to help prevent congenital neurological birth defects.

6 sheets whole wheat lasagna pasta
1 pound ground turkey
2 cups fresh spinach
½ large Spanish onion, chopped
3 – 4 medium garlic cloves, minced
2 tablespoons olive oil
8 ounces low fat cottage cheese
2 cups prepared or homemade tomato sauce
1½ cups part-skim low moisture mozzarella cheese, divided
½ cup reduced fat Parmesan cheese

Preheat the oven to 350°. Boil the pasta approximately 10 minutes with a pinch of salt. Meanwhile, sauté the turkey, spinach, onion, garlic, and olive oil in a large skillet for 20 minutes or until the meat has browned. Drain any excess liquid form the skillet. Coat a 9" x 11" casserole dish with cooking spray. Place 3 sheets of pasta (length wise), lining the bottom of the dish. Layer the turkey mixture, cottage cheese, tomato sauce and mozzarella cheese. Continue to layer ingredients. Place another layer of pasta on top and sprinkle with mozzarella and Parmesan cheese. Bake for 45 minutes.

Whole Wheat Penne with Chicken and Gorgonzola

Serves 4-6

One 12 ounce box whole wheat penne
4 ounces Gorgonzola cheese, crumbled
⅔ cup toasted walnut pieces
½ cup fresh parsley, chopped
¼ cup extra virgin olive oil
1½ teaspoons fresh rosemary, chopped
1 teaspoon garlic
½ teaspoon cracked black pepper to taste
16 ounces chicken, prepared

Cook the penne in water until al dente. Meanwhile, combine the Gorgonzola, walnuts, parsley, oil, rosemary and garlic in a large bowl. Gently stir and season with pepper. Thoroughly drain the penne and toss with the sauce and chicken. Serve hot.

Nutrition Facts
(Per Serving)

Calories	374
Fat Calories	223
Total Fat	24.7g
Saturated Fat	5.9g
Cholesterol	72mg
Sodium	314mg
Total Carbs	7.4g
Fiber	1.3g
Protein	30.5g

Did You Know…

- Nuts are one of nature's most nutrient-rich foods. Walnuts are high in Omega-3 fatty acids.
- Whole wheat pasta contains three times the fiber of white pasta. It is also rated lower than white pasta on the glycemic index. It has been shown to reduce the risk of diabetes, heart disease and some forms of cancer.
- Cheese is a good source of vitamin B12.

Whole Wheat Stuffing

Enjoy this delicious alternative to a traditional stuffing.

Serves 10-12

Nutrition Facts (Per Serving)	
Calories	85
Fat Calories	10
Total Fat	1g
Saturated Fat	0.2g
Cholesterol	0mg
Sodium	198mg
Total Carbs	15.1g
Fiber	2.6g
Protein	3.7g

6 slices of stale whole wheat bread
6 slices of stale white bread
1 cup onion, finely chopped
¾ cup celery, finely chopped
1 teaspoon dried sage
1 teaspoon dried thyme
1 teaspoon dried marjoram
½ teaspoon ground black pepper
2 egg whites, lightly beaten
1 cup of organic low sodium chicken broth

Preheat the oven to 325°.

Tear 8 of the 12 slices of bread into pieces. Place the pieces in a food processor and process into coarse crumbs. This should yield 4 cups. Take the remaining slices and cut into bite size cubes.

Place the bread crumbs and cubes in a large bowl, and add all of the remaining ingredients except the chicken broth. Toss and mix well. Slowly add the broth and continue mixing.

Coat a large casserole dish with a nonstick cooking spray. Spoon the stuffing into the dish, and bake uncovered 45 minutes to an hour.

Did You Know…

- Whole wheat is an excellent source of starchy carbohydrate and dietary fiber.
- Whole wheat is a good source of niacin, riboflavin, and other B vitamins and iron.
- Whole wheat may help prevent heart disease and protect against cancer.
- Whole wheat may help prevent diabetes.

seafood

Blackened Catfish

Serves 4

Four 6-ounce fresh catfish fillets, with skin
3 tablespoons blackened seasoning, prepared; reserve 1 tablespoon
½ cup fresh lemon juice, squeezed
1 tablespoon olive oil
1 tablespoon fresh snipped flat leaf parsley
1 tablespoon cracked black peppercorns

Rinse the fish and place in a zip lock bag. Add the blackened seasoning, lemon juice, olive oil, parsley, and pepper, and shake. Allow the fish to become completely submerged in the marinade and chill for 2 hours. Turn the bag once while the fish is marinating.

Preheat the grill to medium heat. Place the fish, skin side down, in a grill basket that has been coated with cooking spray. Lightly coat the top of the fish with the tablespoon of reserved blackened seasoning. Place the fish on the grill and cook for 12 - 15 minutes or until the fish becomes flakey. Be sure to turn once while grilling. Remove from the grill and discard the skin. Serve warm.

Nutrition Facts
(Per Serving)

Calories	259
Fat Calories	139
Total Fat	15.6g
Saturated Fat	3.3g
Cholesterol	75mg
Sodium	595mg
Total Carbs	5.1g
Fiber	1.3g
Protein	25g

Did You Know…

- Fish may reduce the risk of breast cancer.
- Consuming fish may also reduce the risk of macular degeneration.
- Fish is an excellent source of protein.

Fabulous Fish Tacos

Serves 4

Nutrition Facts (Per Serving)	
Calories	317
Fat Calories	28
Total Fat	3g
Saturated Fat	0.5g
Cholesterol	84mg
Sodium	621mg
Total Carbs	37.9g
Fiber	5.2g
Protein	34.3g

Did You Know...

- Fish may help prevent heart disease and is an excellent source of lean protein.
- Lettuce is a great source of vitamin K and chlorophyll.
- Wheat has shown to help protect against colon cancer.

16 ounces tilapia fillets
1 lemon, juiced
1 tablespoon black pepper
4 whole wheat tortillas, lightly toasted
½ cup Tomatillo Salsa, divided (See recipe page 15)
½ cup cabbage, shredded
⅓ cup reduced fat sour cream, divided
Holy Guacamole (See recipe page 5) optional

Place the tilapia fillets in a freezer bag with the lemon juice and black pepper. Seal the bag and shake. Refrigerate for 3 hours, allowing the fish to marinate. Preheat the grill on low heat. Place the fish in a grill basket and grill on low heat for 8 minutes on each side. Depending on the thickness of the fillet, you may grill slightly longer. Do not overcook or allow the fish to burn. Place the tortillas on the top rack of the grill to keep away from the flame; lightly toast and remove. Place the fish inside the tortillas and top off with fresh Tomatillo Salsa, cabbage and sour cream. Serve warm with Holy Guacamole as an accompaniment, if desired.

Lemon and Dill Tilapia

Serves 4

Four 4-ounce tilapia fillets, thawed
¼ cup lemon juice
1 tablespoon butter, melted
½ teaspoon fresh dill, snipped
½ teaspoon lemon pepper
Butter cooking spray

Preheat oven to 425°. Coat a shallow baking dish with butter spray. Rinse the fillets and pat dry. Place the fillets in the baking dish and drizzle on the lemon juice and melted butter. Generously coat the top of the fish with dill and lemon pepper. Bake at 425° for 9-11 minutes or until fish becomes flakey. Remove from oven and serve warm.

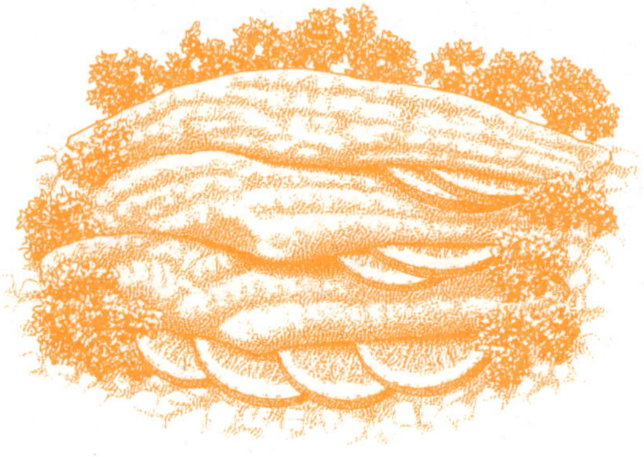

Nutrition Facts

(Per Serving)

Calories	109
Fat Calories	34
Total Fat	3.7g
Saturated Fat	2.2g
Cholesterol	45mg
Sodium	136mg
Total Carbs	1.5g
Fiber	0.1g
Protein	17.4g

Did You Know…

- Fish may lower the risk of chronic ailments such as depression and rheumatoid arthritis.
- Fish may protect against heart disease.
- Dill may help protect the body from carcinogens such as cigarette smoke.

Pecan and Herb Encrusted Grouper

Serves 4

Nutrition Facts (Per Serving)	
Calories	259
Fat Calories	111
Total Fat	12.4g
Saturated Fat	3.3g
Cholesterol	75mg
Sodium	191mg
Total Carbs	2.5g
Fiber	0.7g
Protein	34.3g

Did You Know…

- Eating 10 to 12 ounces of fish per week may reduce the risk of heart disease.
- Pecans are an excellent source of B vitamins.
- Pecans may have a cholesterol lowering effect.

Four 6-ounce fresh Grouper fillets with skin
½ cup finely chopped pecans
2 tablespoons wheat bread crumbs
2 tablespoons butter, softened
2 tablespoons fresh lemon juice
1 tablespoon fresh flat-leaf parsley, snipped
1 tablespoon fresh dill, snipped
1 teaspoon garlic, minced
¼ teaspoon sea salt
Cracked black peppercorns to taste

Preheat the grill to medium heat. Place the pecans in a food processor and pulse until they become fine. In a small bowl, mix the pecans, bread crumbs, butter, lemon juice, parsley, dill, garlic, salt and black pepper. Set aside.

Rinse the fish and pat dry with paper towels. Place the fish, skin side down, in a grill basket that has been coated with cooking spray. Lightly spread the pecan mixture on top of the fish. Grill on medium heat for 12 - 15 minutes, or until fish becomes flakey. Remove from the heat and discard the skin. Serve warm.

Salmon Croquettes

Serves 6

14 ounces canned salmon
2 egg whites
1 egg yolk
½ cup seasoned bread crumbs
¼ cup yellow corn
¼ cup red bell peppers, diced
¼ cup onion, diced
1 teaspoon paprika
1 teaspoon cayenne pepper
½ teaspoon salt
Pepper to taste
¼ cup olive oil

Place the salmon, eggs, bread crumbs, corn, red peppers and onion in a large mixing bowl. Blend in the paprika, cayenne pepper, salt and pepper. Thoroughly mix all the ingredients by hand. Form six croquettes, or patties. Add the olive oil to a skillet and bring to medium heat. Place the croquettes in the skillet and cook for 8 minutes. Allow the croquette to brown before turning, as this prevents it from falling apart. Reduce the heat and cook on low for an additional 20 minutes. Serve warm or cold.

Nutrition Facts
(Per Serving)

Calories	225
Fat Calories	120
Total Fat	13.5g
Saturated Fat	2.3g
Cholesterol	36mg
Sodium	669mg
Total Carbs	9.8g
Fiber	0.9g
Protein	16.4g

Did You Know…

- Salmon is rich in Omega 3 fatty acids.
- It is also an excellent source of potassium, vitamin B12 and selenium.
- Salmon has been proven to be beneficial in the protection against Alzheimer's disease.

Sautéed Mussels

Serves 8

Nutrition Facts (Per Serving)	
Calories	262
Fat Calories	78
Total Fat	8.7g
Saturated Fat	1.5g
Cholesterol	64mg
Sodium	824mg
Total Carbs	17.7g
Fiber	1.4g
Protein	28.4g

Did You Know…

- Mussels are a good source of protein.
- They are also low in calories and fat.

2 tablespoons extra virgin olive oil
⅓ cup fennel, finely chopped
⅓ cup shallots, minced
3 tablespoons garlic, minced
One 14½ ounce can diced tomatoes, drained
1 cup dry white wine
One 8-ounce bottle clam juice
¾ cup water
¼ cup fresh lemon juice
4 pounds mussels, scrubbed and debearded
¼ cup fresh parsley, chopped
Sea salt and cracked black pepper to taste
Lemon wedges to garnish

Heat the oil over medium heat in a large pot with a lid. Add the fennel, shallots, and garlic. Cook, stirring occasionally, until the fennel is tender, about 5 minutes. Add the tomatoes and cook, stirring, 2 minutes. Stir in the wine, clam juice, water, and lemon juice. Add the mussels. Cover and cook, stirring once until the shells open, 5 - 8 minutes.

Ladle broth and mussels into individual bowls. Sprinkle on the parsley. Then, season with salt and pepper. Garnish with lemon wedges.

Note: Always purchase live mussels. Discard mussels that are cracked or do not open after they have been cooked.

Sea Scallops and Corn Salad

Serves 6 to 8

One 15¼ ounce can of corn, drained
1 pint grape tomatoes, halved
¼ cup scallions, thinly sliced
⅓ cup basil leaves, finely chopped
1 teaspoon shallots, minced
2 tablespoons balsamic vinegar
2 tablespoons hot water
1½ teaspoons Dijon mustard
¼ cup plus 3 tablespoons safflower oil
Sea salt and cracked black pepper to taste
1½ pounds medium sea scallops (about 30)

In a large saucepan of boiling water, cook the corn, tomatoes, scallions and basil for 5 - 8 minutes. Drain and place in a large mixing bowl.

For the Vinaigrette: In a food processor, purée the shallot with the vinegar, hot water and mustard. With the food processor on, slowly add 6 tablespoons of the safflower oil until combined. Add salt and pepper to taste.

Toss the corn salad with the vinaigrette.

In a large bowl, toss the remaining 1 tablespoon of oil with the scallops; season with salt and pepper. Place half the scallops in a large pan and cook over moderately high heat, turning once, until browned, about 4 minutes per batch.

To serve: Place the corn salad on plates and top with the scallops.

Nutrition Facts
(Per Serving)

Calories	197
Fat Calories	59
Total Fat	6.5g
Saturated Fat	0.6g
Cholesterol	28mg
Sodium	152mg
Total Carbs	18.2g
Fiber	2g
Protein	16.4g

Did You Know…

- Corn is a good source of folate and thiamine.
- Scallops are a great source of protein and are rich in vitamin B12.
- Safflower oil is considered a dietary oil because it contains mono and or poly unsaturated fats with very low levels of saturated fats.
- Safflower oil also makes it possible to absorb fat soluble vitamins such as A, D, E, and K.
- Tomatoes may block the effects of environmental toxins with a compound they contain, Chlorogenic Acid.

Tasty Tuna Melt

Serves 2

Nutrition Facts (Per Serving)	
Calories	449
Fat Calories	135
Total Fat	15g
Saturated Fat	4.4g
Cholesterol	68mg
Sodium	785mg
Total Carbs	41.3g
Fiber	5.9g
Protein	37.1g

Did You Know...

- Consuming fish may help reduce the risk of breast cancer.
- Multi grain bread is a good source of fiber.
- Turkey bacon is leaner than pork bacon and has significantly less amounts of fat.

Tuna Salad (See recipe page 36)
Two slices tomato
Two slices reduced fat Swiss cheese
4 slices turkey bacon
4 slices multi grain bread

Prepare the tuna salad and spread it on two slices of bread. Place one slice of tomato on each sandwich. Add two slices of turkey bacon to each sandwich. Top the bacon with one slice of Swiss cheese and the remaining bread. Toast the sandwiches in a toaster oven for up to five minutes or in a 350° oven until the cheese has melted, about 5 – 10 minutes. (The cheese may get a little messy, but will be delicious). Serve warm.

Tuna Steak Sandwiches

Serves 4

Four 4-ounce tuna steaks
½ purple onion, sliced
½ tomato, sliced
¼ head Romaine lettuce
Chipotle sauce (see recipe below)
4 whole wheat round buns

Nutrition Facts (Per Serving)	
Calories	351
Fat Calories	111
Total Fat	12.3g
Saturated Fat	1.9g
Cholesterol	73mg
Sodium	573mg
Total Carbs	23.2g
Fiber	2.9g
Protein	36.7g

Chipotle Sauce

Yields ¾ cup

½ cup reduced fat mayonnaise
3 tablespoons canned chipotle peppers in Adobo sauce
1 tablespoon fresh lemon juice

Preheat the grill to medium heat. Place the tuna steaks in a fish basket and place on the grill. The fish basket will ensure that the fish doesn't fall apart when turning over the fish. Grill 4 - 6 minutes per ½ inch thickness. Turn frequently and do not overcook. Meanwhile, slice the onion and tomato. Remove 4 leaves from the head of the Romaine, and set aside in the refrigerator.

For the Chipotle Sauce: Place the mayonnaise, chipotle peppers and lemon juice in a food processor. Blend for 30 - 60 seconds or until the ingredients form a sauce. Remove and chill.

Place the buns on the grill for 3 - 4 minutes, away from the flame. and lightly toast. Remove the fish and the buns from the grill. Once the buns have cooled, brush on the chipotle sauce and add the tuna steaks, onion, tomato and lettuce. Serve warm.

Did You Know...

- Fish has been touted to prevent heart disease.
- Omega 3 fatty acids are found in tuna.
- Fish consumption may lower the risk of breast cancer.

side dishes

Baked Beans

Serves 6-8

28 ounce can of beans in tomato sauce
¼ cup ketchup
2 teaspoons yellow mustard, prepared
3 tablespoons brown sugar Splenda
⅓ cup onions, chopped
3 slices turkey bacon, crumbled (optional)

Combine beans, ketchup, mustard, Splenda and onions in a casserole dish. Bake for 45 minutes at 350°. Remove and serve warm or cold.

Nutrition Facts
(Per Serving)

Calories	158
Fat Calories	13
Total Fat	1.4g
Saturated Fat	0.5g
Cholesterol	9mg
Sodium	603mg
Total Carbs	29.2g
Fiber	6.7g
Protein	7.1g

Did You Know...

- Beans contain folate and vitamins A and C.
- Beans are high in protein and iron.
- Onions may aid in the prevention of tumor growth.

Couscous

Yields 2 cups

Nutrition Facts (Per Serving)	
Calories	219
Fat Calories	51
Total Fat	5.7g
Saturated Fat	0.9g
Cholesterol	0mg
Sodium	224mg
Total Carbs	35.8
Fiber	2.8g
Protein	6.2g

Did You Know…

- Whole grains are nutritious because they are low in calories and high in fiber.
- Grains are also a great source of complex carbohydrates.
- Carrots are rich in antioxidants that may help to prevent cardiovascular disease.

1 cup whole wheat couscous
1½ tablespoon peanut oil
1½ cups organic chicken broth
½ cup carrots, chopped
1 teaspoon curry, ground
Pinch of salt
Cracked black pepper to taste
Garnish with chopped green onions

Heat oil in a medium saucepan. Add the couscous and lightly brown on medium heat. Add the chicken broth, carrots, curry, and salt. Bring to a boil. Remove from heat cover and let stand for 5-8 minutes. Place on serving dish and add a dash of black peppercorns. Garnish with green onions.

Creamy Cauliflower

Serves 4

4 cups cauliflower florets
1 tablespoon butter
1 ounce 2% milk
1 tablespoon chives, chopped
Pinch of salt
White pepper to taste

Steam the cauliflower for 8 - 10 minutes or until soft. Drain and place the cauliflower in a food processor. Add the butter, milk, chives, salt, and pepper. Pulse until the desired consistency is achieved. Serve warm.

Nutrition Facts

(Per Serving)

Calories	63
Fat Calories	31
Total Fat	3.4g
Saturated Fat	1.9g
Cholesterol	8mg
Sodium	318mg
Total Carbs	5.6g
Fiber	3.4g
Protein	2.5g

Did You Know…

- Cauliflower is a great source of vitamin K.
- Cauliflower is rich in B vitamins, phosphorus, potassium and fiber.
- The trace mineral boron is found in cauliflower.

Fiesta Cornbread

Serves 6

Nutrition Facts
(Per Serving)

Calories	258
Fat Calories	158
Total Fat	17.5g
Saturated Fat	3.1g
Cholesterol	11mg
Sodium	594mg
Total Carbs	20.8g
Fiber	1.9g
Protein	4.1g

Did You Know...

- Yellow corn has valuable amounts of lutein. Lutein has been associated with reducing the risk of macular degeneration.
- Corn is a rich source of vitamin B1.
- Egg whites are great source of protein.

8 ounces creamed corn
8 ounces reduced fat sour cream
1 cup self rising corn meal
½ cup canola oil, reserving 2 tablespoons
4 egg whites
8 ounces green chilies
½ cup reduced fat cheddar cheese

Place a cast iron skillet in oven and preheat to 400°. Once the oven has reached 400°, remove the skillet from the heat and coat with two tablespoons of canola oil. Mix the creamed corn, sour cream, corn meal, canola oil, egg whites, chilies and cheese in a large mixing bowl. Stir until thoroughly blended. Pour the mixture into the cast iron skillet and bake for 25 - 30 minutes. Remove from oven. Let stand and cool. Use a butter knife to loosen the bread from the skillet and turn the skillet over to release the cornbread. Serve warm.

Ginger Garlic Greens

Serves 4

1 tablespoon canola oil
1 teaspoon garlic, chopped
1 teaspoon fresh ginger, chopped
¼ cup scallions, sliced
½ cup carrots, shredded
One 16-ounce bag baby spinach
1 tablespoon reduced sodium soy sauce
½ teaspoon dark sesame oil
Cracked black pepper to taste

Heat the canola oil in a heavy saucepan over medium high heat. Add the garlic and ginger. Cook, stirring, until fragrant but not browned, about 30 seconds. Add the scallions, carrots and spinach in batches, tossing with tongs. Stir-fry until wilted and softened, 2 - 3 minutes longer. Add the soy sauce, sesame oil and pepper. Toss and serve.

Nutrition Facts (Per Serving)	
Calories	84
Fat Calories	40
Total Fat	4.4g
Saturated Fat	0.4g
Cholesterol	0mg
Sodium	346mg
Total Carbs	7g
Fiber	3.8g
Protein	4.1g

Did You Know…

- Spinach contains almost twice as much iron as other green vegetables.
- Spinach is an alkaline food source that helps to regulate body pH.
- Carrots may help to protect against cancer and cardiovascular disease.

Grilled Squash and Zucchini

Serves 4

Nutrition Facts (Per Serving)	
Calories	100
Fat Calories	62
Total Fat	6.9g
Saturated Fat	1g
Cholesterol	0mg
Sodium	312mg
Total Carbs	8.2g
Fiber	2.6g
Protein	1.5g

Did You Know...

- Squash is 95% percent water, which may help to keep the body hydrated.
- Summer squash contains fair amounts of vitamin C, carotenes and potassium.
- The carotenes found in squash may help protect against sun damage to the body.

1 large summer squash
1 large zucchini
1 medium onion
¼ cup fresh parsley, chopped
¼ cup olive oil
1 teaspoon sea salt
Cracked black peppercorn to taste

Preheat the grill on medium to low heat. Cut the yellow squash, zucchini and onion into cubes and set aside in a large mixing bowl. Add the parsley, olive oil, salt and pepper. Mix and coat the vegetables. Place the vegetables in aluminum foil and seal tightly. Place the vegetables on the grill and grill for 25 minutes. Serve warm.

Oven Roasted Potatoes

1 pound red potatoes
¼ cup olive oil
½ cup chopped onion
½ cup chopped green bell pepper
2 garlic cloves, minced
1 teaspoon salt
Cracked black pepper to taste
⅓ cup Parmesan cheese

Preheat the oven to 350°. Scrub the potatoes and cut into cubes. Place the potatoes in a 9" x 11" baking dish. Coat with the olive oil and toss. Add the onion and green pepper to the potatoes. Sprinkle the garlic, salt and pepper over the potatoes. Bake for 35 minutes. Remove the potatoes from the oven and sprinkle with the cheese. Bake 10 minutes or until cheese has melted.

Serves 6 - 8

Nutrition Facts
(Per Serving)

Calories	162
Fat Calories	74
Total Fat	8.1g
Saturated Fat	1.7g
Cholesterol	3mg
Sodium	83mg
Total Carbs	18.4g
Fiber	1.8g
Protein	3.9g

Did You Know...

- Potatoes are low in calories and rich in fiber.
- Red potatoes are rated lower than white potatoes on the glycemic index.
- Potatoes contain the essential amino acid Lysine.

Rosemary Mashed Potatoes

Serves 8

Nutrition Facts (Per Serving)	
Calories	97
Fat Calories	19
Total Fat	2.1g
Saturated Fat	1.2g
Cholesterol	6mg
Sodium	150mg
Total Carbs	15.2g
Fiber	3g
Protein	4.2g

Did You Know…

- Consuming potatoes with skin provides more complex carbohydrates.
- Potatoes contain valuable amounts of vitamin C and fiber.
- Rosemary may stimulate the immune system and improve circulation. It also has been shown to be effective in easing inflammatory conditions such as rheumatoid arthritis.

⅔ cup no-salt, fat-free chicken broth
2 tablespoons fresh rosemary, chopped
2 pounds Yukon Gold potatoes, quartered
½ cup low fat sour cream
1 teaspoon Dijon mustard
1 teaspoon sea salt
White pepper to taste

Place the broth and rosemary in a small saucepan and simmer on medium heat for 10 minutes. Remove from heat, cover and set broth aside. Peel the potatoes lightly, leaving some of the skin, and quarter them. Place the potatoes in a large saucepan and add 5 cups of water, covering the potatoes. Cook on medium to high heat, and simmer until the potatoes are tender, for 20 – 25 minutes. Drain and place the potatoes in a large bowl. Beat with an electric mixer at medium speed. Add the broth and rosemary to the potatoes. Add the sour cream, mustard and salt. Place the mixture in a medium bowl and sprinkle with white pepper before serving.

Sautéed Mushrooms

Makes ¾ cup

8 ounces button mushrooms, whole
¼ cup Worcestershire sauce
1 tablespoon olive oil
1 teaspoon shallots, minced
2 teaspoons garlic, minced
1 teaspoon cracked black pepper
Fresh flat leaf parsley to garnish

Rinse the mushrooms. Place them in a saucepan with the Worcestershire sauce, oil, shallots, garlic and pepper. Cover and simmer on low heat for 12 - 15 minutes. Remove from the heat. Place in a serving dish with the sauce. Sprinkle on the parsley. Serve warm.

Nutrition Facts
(Per Serving)

Calories	33
Fat Calories	13
Total Fat	1.3g
Saturated Fat	0.2g
Cholesterol	0mg
Sodium	83mg
Total Carbs	3.5g
Fiber	0.9g
Protein	1.4g

Did You Know...

- Mushrooms are an excellent source of minerals.
- Mushrooms are also a great source of B vitamins.
- Consuming mushrooms may reduce the risk of cancer.

Steamed Green Beans

Serves 4

Nutrition Facts (Per Serving)	
Calories	70
Fat Calories	32
Total Fat	3.7g
Saturated Fat	0.3g
Cholesterol	0mg
Sodium	151mg
Total Carbs	7g
Fiber	3.1g
Protein	2.6g

Did You Know…

- Beans are best known for their cholesterol lowering fiber content.
- Beans contain a significant amount of antioxidants.
- Beans also have been touted as keeping the heart healthy.

2 cups fresh snap green beans, whole
½ cup red pepper, thinly sliced
1 tablespoon fresh lemon juice
⅓ cup almonds, slivered
Pinch of sea salt
Cracked black pepper to taste

Place the green beans and red pepper in a sauce pan with water and lemon juice. Steam the vegetables on medium heat for 5 minutes, or until tender. Meanwhile, toast the almonds in a small skillet for 4 - 5 minutes, until slightly brown and fragrant. Remove the vegetables from the heat and drain. Sprinkle on the toasted almonds and salt and pepper. Serve warm.

Traditional Mashed Potatoes

Leave the skin on for additional nutritional value.

6 medium red potatoes
¾ cup 2% milk
¼ teaspoon black pepper
2 tablespoons butter
2 tablespoons chives (optional)
Salt to taste

Cut the potatoes into 1" chunks and place in a saucepan with water and a pinch of salt. Bring to a boil over medium heat for approximately 20 - 25 minutes. Drain the potatoes and return to the pan. Add the milk, pepper, butter and chives. Mix with a mixer until the potatoes reach the desired consistency. Season with salt to taste.

Serves 6

Nutrition Facts
(Per Serving)

Calories 151

Fat Calories 41

Total Fat 4.5g

Saturated Fat 2.8g

Cholesterol 12mg

Sodium 26mg

Total Carbs 23.9g

Fiber 2g

Protein 3.7g

Did You Know…

- The skin of a red potato is rich in fiber.
- Red potatoes are rated low on the glycemic index which makes them an excellent choice for weight loss and blood sugar stabilization.

vegan @ vegetarian

Angel Hair Pasta with Sun Dried Tomato Pesto

The pesto may be refrigerated for up to two days or frozen for one month.

1 tablespoon pine nuts
¾ cup low-fat, low-sodium chicken or vegetable broth
½ cup sun-dried tomatoes, not in oil, coarsely chopped
3 medium cloves garlic
¼ cup Parmesan cheese, grated
½ cup lightly packed basil leaves
1 tablespoon fresh lemon juice

1 pound whole wheat angel hair pasta

To toast the pine nuts, toss them in a skillet until slightly browned and fragrant.

In a small saucepan, bring the broth to a boil. Remove from the heat and add the tomatoes to the pan. Cover and let stand until the tomatoes are soft and have cooled for approximately 30 minutes. Drain, reserving 3 tablespoons of the liquid.

Place the tomatoes in a food processor. Slowly add the garlic cloves and pine nuts, and process until all of the ingredients are finely chopped. Add the cheese, basil and lemon juice. Process the mixture for about 10 seconds. Finally, add the reserved tomato liquid and process until smooth

Add a pinch of salt and olive oil to a pot of water. Bring to a boil and add the pasta. Boil until the pasta is al dente. Drain and toss with the pesto. Serve immediately.

Serves 6

Nutrition Facts

Calories 148
Fat Calories 24
Total Fat 2.6g
Saturated Fat 1g
Cholesterol 5mg
Sodium 270mg
Total Carbs 23.9g
Fiber 4.2g
Protein 7g

Did You Know…

- Pine nuts are high in monounsaturated fat and arginine.
- Pine nuts are also a great source of potassium and magnesium.
- Tomatoes are a good source of dietary fiber.

Baked Eggplant

Serves 6

Nutrition Facts (Per Serving)	
Calories	121
Fat Calories	80
Total Fat	8.9g
Saturated Fat	3.5g
Cholesterol	11mg
Sodium	272mg
Total Carbs	6.3g
Fiber	2.1g
Protein	4g

Did You Know...

- Eggplant is an excellent source of fiber, vitamins B1 and B6, and potassium.
- The skin of the eggplant contains Nasunin, an anthocyanin flavonoid. Nasunin is considered a free radical scavenger that may help protect cell membranes from damage.
- Eggplant may help lower cholesterol levels.

1 medium eggplant
1 large red pepper
⅛ cup olive oil
1 large garlic clove, minced
3 ounces goat cheese, crumbled (optional)
½ teaspoon sea salt
Cracked black pepper to taste

Preheat the oven to 350°. Slice the eggplant into ½" thick slices. Cut red pepper lengthwise into 6 strips. Spray a 9" x 11" shallow baking dish with olive oil. Place the eggplant in the dish and drizzle on the olive oil. Sprinkle on the garlic, cheese and salt. Layer the red pepper slices on top of the eggplant. Add the black pepper to taste. Bake for 35 minutes and serve warm.

Brown Rice and Veggies

Serves 6

½ cup cooked brown rice
½ cup carrots, diced
½ cup broccoli florets
¼ cup yellow squash, diced
¼ cup zucchini, diced
¼ cup peas
¼ cup corn
¼ cup red onion, chopped

Marinade and Dressing

4 tablespoons red wine vinegar
2 tablespoons apple cider vinegar
2 teaspoons Grey Poupon mustard
2 teaspoons Splenda
½ teaspoon salt
½ teaspoon pepper
4 tablespoons olive oil

To prepare the marinade and dressing: In a large measuring cup, combine the red wine vinegar, apple cider vinegar, mustard, Splenda, salt and pepper; mix together. Slowly add the olive oil until the dressing is emulsified.

Place the brown rice in a large bowl. Add the carrots, broccoli, squash, zucchini, peas, corn, and onion. Toss gently. Pour the marinade over the veggies and toss gently. Refrigerate overnight. Serve cold.

Nutrition Facts
(Per Serving)

Calories	103
Fat Calories	52
Total Fat	5.8g
Saturated Fat	0.8g
Cholesterol	0mg
Sodium	137mg
Total Carbs	11.4g
Fiber	1.4g
Protein	1.4g

Did You Know...

- Brown rice is rich in B vitamins. Consuming brown rice may be helpful in lowering cholesterol.
- Carrots are rich in beta carotene. Beta carotene may help reduce the risk of lung cancer.
- Peas are a good source of protein.

vegan & vegetarian

Greek Pizza

Serves 4

Nutrition Facts (Per Serving)	
Calories	265
Fat Calories	123
Total Fat	13.7g
Saturated Fat	6g
Cholesterol	6mg
Sodium	780mg
Total Carbs	24.3g
Fiber	4.8g
Protein	11.3g

4 whole wheat flour tortillas
½ cup hummus (See recipe page 7)
½ cup bottled roasted red sweet peppers, drained and chopped
½ cup feta cheese, crumbled
½ cup low moisture part skim mozzarella cheese, shredded
8 kalamata olives, pitted and halved
2 tablespoons fresh oregano, snipped

Preheat the oven to 425°. Arrange the tortillas in an even layer on a very large baking sheet. Bake for 3 - 4 minutes or until crisp.

Spread the tortillas with hummus; top with roasted peppers, feta cheese, and mozzarella. Bake about 6 minutes or until the cheese is melted and the edges of the tortillas are lightly browned. Top with the olives and oregano. Quarter each pizza and serve warm.

Did You Know...

- Cheese has been known to help protect against dental cavities by supporting plague PH.
- Cheese may help protect against or delay the onset of osteoporosis.
- Olives may be helpful in the treatment of asthma and arthritis.
- Oregano contains two very powerful antimicrobial agents, Thymol and Carvacrol.

Grilled Portobellos

Serves 4

Four 6-8 ounce fresh portobello mushrooms, sliced
2 tablespoons balsamic vinegar
1 tablespoon red wine vinegar
1 tablespoon olive oil
¼ teaspoons cracked black pepper
¼ teaspoon salt

Lightly rinse the mushroom caps and gently pat dry with paper towels. In a small bowl, combine the balsamic vinegar, red wine vinegar, oil, cracked black pepper and salt. Brush both sides of the mushrooms with the vinegar mixture.

Place the mushrooms on the rack of an uncovered grill directly over medium heat. Grill for 8 - 10 minutes or just until the mushrooms are tender, turning and brushing once with the remaining vinegar mixture halfway through grilling.

Nutrition Facts
(Per Serving)

Calories	57
Fat Calories	33
Total Fat	3.6g
Saturated Fat	0.5g
Cholesterol	0mg
Sodium	153mg
Total Carbs	4.9g
Fiber	0.8g
Protein	1.2g

Did You Know...

- Portobello mushrooms are a great source of vitamins B12 and B6.
- Mushrooms contain phytochemicals that may help prevent cancer.

Homemade Granola

Makes 10 servings

Nutrition Facts
(Per Serving)

Calories	294
Fat Calories	66
Total Fat	7.4g
Saturated Fat	2.3g
Cholesterol	0mg
Sodium	20mg
Total Carbs	48.6g
Fiber	5.6g
Protein	8.3g

Did You Know...

- Oatmeal is an excellent source of soluble fiber.
- Oatmeal is a great source of calcium, manganese and other B vitamins.
- Eating oatmeal may help reduce blood cholesterol levels.
- Coconut is a good source of iron and fiber and is high in easy to digest fatty acids.
- Raisins are a rich source of vitamin C, iron and potassium.
- Cinnamon may aid in the relief of heartburn.

This granola is great for a snack or served as a breakfast cereal with vanilla soymilk.

Vegetable oil spray
2½ cups uncooked regular or quick cooking rolled oats
½ cup sweetened shredded coconut
½ cup sliced natural unblanched almonds
¼ cup raw sunflower seeds
¼ cup honey
¼ cup molasses
½ teaspoon ground cinnamon
½ cup brown raisins
½ cup cranberries
1 teaspoon vanilla extract

Preheat the oven to 325°. Spray a 10" x 15" pan with vegetable oil spray. In a large bowl, combine the oats, coconut, almonds, and sunflower seeds. In a small bowl, blend the honey, molasses, and cinnamon with 3 tablespoons of hot water. Pour the liquid over the oat mixture and use your hands to combine the mixture until the dry ingredients are evenly coated with the honey and molasses. Transfer to the baking sheet, spreading out an even layer. Bake, stirring thoroughly every 5 minutes, until the granola turns a rich, dark brown, 30 - 35 minutes. Remove from the oven, stir in the raisins, cranberries and vanilla, and let cool completely. The granola will crisp as it cools. Transfer to an airtight container and store at room temperature.

Margherita Pita Pizza

Serves 8

- 2 teaspoons olive oil
- 1 teaspoon oregano
- 1 teaspoon balsamic vinegar
- 1 garlic clove, pressed
- 4 flat whole wheat pita bread rounds (without pockets)
- 2 Roma tomatoes, diced
- ½ cup part-skim mozzarella cheese, shredded
- 2 tablespoons fresh basil leaves, snipped

Preheat the oven to 425°. In a small bowl, combine the olive oil, oregano, vinegar and garlic; mix well. Place the pita rounds on a baking pan. Brush one side of each pita round with the oil mixture.

Slice the tomatoes. Top the pita rounds evenly with tomatoes and cheese. Bake 10-12 minutes in a toaster oven until the cheese has melted and the edges are lightly browned. Sprinkle generously with basil. Cut pizzas into quarters. Serve warm.

Nutrition Facts

(Per Serving)

Calories	149
Fat Calories	51
Total Fat	5.7g
Saturated Fat	1.4g
Cholesterol	4mg
Sodium	216mg
Total Carbs	19g
Fiber	2.7g
Protein	5.6g

Did You Know…

- Wheat has been shown to reduce the risk of breast cancer by decreasing blood estrogen which has been known to promote breast cancer.
- Basil and oregano are members of the mint family. Basil has been used in the treatment of kidney aliments. Oregano has very powerful antioxidant activity.
- Garlic has antibacterial properties.

Spaghetti Squash with Mushroom and Tomato Sauce

Serves 6

Nutrition Facts (Per Serving)	
Calories	265
Fat Calories	38
Total Fat	4.1g
Saturated Fat	0.5g
Cholesterol	0mg
Sodium	981mg
Total Carbs	49.4g
Fiber	10.7g
Protein	7.5g

Did You Know…

- Winter squash is high in fiber.
- Squash is an excellent source of carotenes and vitamin C.
- It is also a good source of vitamin B1 pantothenic acid, folic acid, and potassium.

4 pounds spaghetti squash
2 ounces dried porcini mushrooms
1 cup boiling water
3 cups Italian Tomato Sauce (See recipe page 118)

Preheat the oven to 350°.

Prick the spaghetti squash four or five times with a fork. Place the squash on a rimmed baking sheet, and bake 1 ½ hours until soft. Remove from oven and let stand and cool.

Meanwhile, place the dried mushrooms in a medium bowl and cover them with the boiling water. Set aside to soften for about 15 minutes. Drain the mushrooms, reserving the liquid they soaked in. If the liquid is sandy, pass it through a colander lined with cheesecloth or two sheets of paper towels to strain it.

Chop the mushrooms, discarding the tough stems. Place the mushrooms and the strained liquid in a medium saucepan set over medium heat. Bring to a simmer, and then reduce heat to low and cook until the liquid has reduced by half, about 5 minutes. Stir in the Italian Tomato Sauce and cook until heated thoroughly. Cover and set aside to keep warm.

Once the squash is soft, cut the squash in half; scrape out the seeds and discard. Use a fork to shred pulp into its natural threads, letting them fall into a large bowl. (You should have about 6 cups of squash threads.) Add the sauce, toss well, and serve.

Tofu Italian Style

The tofu will take on the flavor of this delicious dish. Don't forget to press and blot the tofu dry. Removing as much moisture as possible will ensure a crispier crust. Let the tofu stand while you assemble the remaining ingredients. Tofu is great for a vegetarian or vegan diet.

1½ pounds extra-firm tofu, cut crosswise into 8 slices
3 tablespoons olive oil
2 cups red bell peppers, thinly sliced
8 ounces button or cremini mushrooms, sliced
2 teaspoons garlic, minced
½ teaspoon sea salt
¼ teaspoon red pepper flakes
1 tablespoon black olives, sliced
¼ cup chopped fresh basil
Cracked black pepper to taste

Set the tofu on a plate lined with a double layer of paper towels. Top with more paper towels and another plate. Then, place a can on top of the plate so that the sides of the tofu bulge slightly. Add pressure and let stand 5 - 10 minutes. Then pour off and discard the liquid. Pat dry with clean paper towels.

Heat 1 tablespoon of the oil in a large nonstick skillet over medium high heat. Add the tofu and cook until golden, 3 - 4 minutes per side. Transfer to plates and keep warm in a 200° oven.

Heat the remaining 2 tablespoons of oil in a skillet over medium heat. Add the peppers and cook until softened, about 5 minutes. Add the mushrooms, garlic, salt, red pepper flakes, and olives. Cover and cook until the mushrooms begin to release their liquid, about 3 minutes. Uncover, increase the heat to high, and cook until almost all of the liquid has evaporated, about 3 minutes longer. Stir in the basil and black pepper. Divide the vegetables and the tofu and serve.

Serves 4

Nutrition Facts
(Per Serving)

Calories 347
Fat calories 169
Total Fat 18.9g
Saturated Fat 2.7g
Cholesterol 0mg
Sodium 340mg
Total Carbs 15.5g
Fiber 6.3g
Protein 29g

Did You Know...

- Tofu is puréed soy beans made into the form of a cake.
- Tofu is a great source of high quality protein, iron, B vitamins, potassium, zinc and other minerals.
- Tofu is low in calories and saturated fat.
- Red peppers are an excellent source of beta carotene and vitamin C.
- Beta carotene found in red peppers may help prevent cancer.
- Mushrooms are fat free and very low in calories. They are also rich in minerals.
- Basil can be used as a tonic or cold remedy.

Vegetable Quiche

Serves 6 - 8

Nutrition Facts
(Per Serving)

Calories	172
Fat Calories	78
Total Fat	8.9g
Saturated Fat	2.6g
Cholesterol	110mg
Sodium	401mg
Total Carbs	6.7g
Fiber	0.5g
Protein	16.7g

Did You Know...

- Eggs are a great source of thiamine, biotin and B12.
- Try eliminating some of the yolks when preparing eggs. This will reduce the amount of cholesterol ingested.
- Eggs contain betaine. Betaine may reduce the levels of homocysteine that can damage blood vessels.

2 tablespoons olive oil
½ cup onion, diced
½ cup mushrooms, sliced
½ cup red pepper, diced
9 egg whites
3 whole eggs
1½ cups non fat milk
⅓ cup Parmesan cheese
Salt and pepper to taste

Preheat oven to 350°. Place the olive oil, onion, mushrooms and red pepper in a skillet and sauté for 8 - 10 minutes. Remove and drain. Whisk the eggs and milk in a bowl and set aside. Spray a 9" x 11" baking dish with cooking spray. Place the vegetables in the baking dish and cover with the egg mixture. Bake for 35 minutes. Remove from the oven and generously sprinkle on the cheese and salt and pepper. Bake for an additional 10 minutes or until thoroughly done. Remove from the oven and serve warm.

Vegetarian Vegetable Soup

Serves 6

2 bay leaves
32 ounces prepared low sodium vegetable juice
8 ounces stewed tomatoes
15 ounces frozen peas
1 cup carrots, sliced
15 ounces frozen corn
15 ounces frozen French green beans
¼ cup onion, chopped
¼ cup celery, chopped
1 teaspoon oregano
1 teaspoon marjoram
1 teaspoon black pepper

Tie up the bay leaves in a cheesecloth bag. Place the vegetable juice in a stock pot. Add the stewed tomatoes, peas, carrots, corn, green beans, onion, celery, oregano, bay leaves, marjoram and black pepper. Bring to a boil. Reduce the heat and cover for 35 minutes. Cook until the vegetables are tender. Remove the bay leaves. Serve warm.

Nutrition Facts
(Per Serving)

Calories 191
Fat Calories 11
Total Fat 1.2g
Saturated Fat 0.1g
Cholesterol 0mg
Sodium 870mg
Total Carbs 38g
Fiber 8.1g
Protein 6.9g

Did You Know…

- Vegetables are an excellent source of dietary fiber.
- Vegetables are also a rich source of complex carbohydrates.
- Consuming vegetables may reduce the risks of cancer and many other diseases.

dressings and sauces

Barbecue Sauce

Yields 1¼ cups

- 1 cup catsup
- ½ cup water
- ⅓ cup white vinegar
- 2 tablespoons Worcestershire sauce
- ¼ cup Splenda brown sugar
- 1 tablespoon dried onion
- 1 teaspoon cayenne pepper
- ¼ teaspoon salt

Mix together all the ingredients in a bowl and refrigerate.

Nutrition Facts (Per Serving)	
Calories	68
Fat Calories	1
Total Fat	0.2g
Saturated Fat	0g
Cholesterol	0mg
Sodium	29mg
Total Carbs	16.1g
Fiber	0.5g
Protein	0.5g

Did You Know…

- Catsup is very low in calories.
- Cayenne pepper may have thermogenic properties.

Basil Mayonnaise

Yields 1¼ cups

Nutrition Facts (Per Serving)	
Calories	82
Fat Calories	61
Total Fat	6.7g
Saturated Fat	1.9g
Cholesterol	10mg
Sodium	184mg
Total Carbs	4.6g
Fiber	0.1g
Protein	0.6g

Did You Know…

- Basil may help improve poor circulation.
- Basil has been touted to be an anti-cancer herb.
- Many dairy foods are good sources of protein.

½ cup reduced fat mayonnaise
½ cup reduced fat sour cream
1 tablespoon fresh lemon juice
¼ cup fresh basil, chopped
¼ teaspoon white pepper
Pinch of salt

Place the mayonnaise, sour cream, lemon juice, basil, pepper and salt in a food processor and pulse for 30 seconds or until the desired consistency is achieved. Chill and serve.

Chipotle Sauce

Yields ¾ cup

½ cup reduced fat mayonnaise
3 tablespoons canned chipotle peppers in Adobo sauce
1 tablespoon fresh lemon juice, squeezed

Place the mayonnaise, chipotle peppers and lemon juice in a food processor. Blend for 30 - 60 seconds or until the ingredients form a sauce. Remove and chill.

Nutrition Facts
(Per Serving)

Calories	61
Fat Calories	44
Total Fat	4.9g
Saturated Fat	0.7g
Cholesterol	4mg
Sodium	188mg
Total Carbs	4g
Fiber	0.1g
Protein	0.2g

Did You Know...

- Hot peppers may help alleviate nasal congestion.
- Removing the peppers' seeds may produce a milder flavor.
- Peppers may prevent blood clots that can lead to heart attacks and stroke.

Cocktail Sauce

Yields 1¼ cups

Nutrition Facts (Per Serving)
Calories 39
Fat Calories 1
Total Fat 0.1g
Saturated Fat 0g
Cholesterol 0g
Sodium 48mg
Total Carbs 8.9g
Fiber 0.5g
Protein 0.5g

Did You Know…

- Horseradish may alleviate nasal and sinus congestion.
- Lemon juice has been touted to have antiviral properties.

1 cup ketchup
2 - 3 tablespoons prepared horseradish
2 tablespoons fresh lemon juice
1 teaspoon capers, drained
2 tablespoons Worcestershire sauce

Place the ketchup, horseradish, lemon juice, capers and Worcestershire sauce in a mixing bowl and blend together. Serve chilled.

Dill Sauce

Yields 1 cup

8 ounces lowfat plain organic yogurt
1½ tablespoons fresh dill, chopped (to taste)
1 tablespoon fresh lemon juice
1 teaspoon garlic, pressed
1 teaspoon capers, drained (optional)
½ teaspoon white pepper
Pinch of sea salt

In a mixing bowl, combine the yogurt, dill, lemon juice, garlic, capers, white pepper and salt. Blend thoroughly. Serve chilled.

Nutrition Facts
(Per Serving)

Calories	23
Fat Calories	1
Total Fat	0.1g
Saturated Fat	0g
Cholesterol	1mg
Sodium	29mg
Total Carbs	3.4g
Fiber	0.1g
Protein	2.2g

Did You Know…

- Yogurt may help to maintain normal intestinal micro flora balance.
- Yogurt may reduce the risk of colon cancer.
- Dill helps to promote the detoxification of the liver by eliminating toxins.

Italian Tomato Gravy

Serves 6

Nutrition Facts (Per Serving)	
Calories	159
Fat Calories	72
Total fat	8.1g
Saturated Fat	2.3g
Cholesterol	7mg
Sodium	250mg
Total Carbs	15.2g
Fiber	2.5g
Protein	6.3g

Did You Know…

- Tomatoes are a great source of vitamin C, beta carotene, folate, and potassium.
- Tomatoes are also a great source of lycopene, an antioxidant that has been known to fight or ward off certain cancers. Lycopene is found in the skin of the tomato. The deeper the color of the tomato, the more nutritionally dense it is.
- Wheat pasta contains three times the amount of fiber as white pasta. It is also rated lower than white pasta on the glycemic index.
- Garlic may help prevent or lower blood pressure and elevated blood cholesterol levels.

2 - 3 tablespoons olive oil
5 large garlic cloves, minced
24 ounces stewed tomatoes
1 small can tomato paste
½ cup dry red wine
1 tablespoon oregano
1 tablespoon basil
1 tablespoon red pepper flakes
¼ cup black olives, minced
½ cup Parmesan cheese, grated
1 pound whole wheat angel hair pasta

Heat the olive oil in a sauce pan and add the garlic. Brown the garlic for approximately two minutes. Add the tomatoes, tomato paste, wine, oregano, basil, red pepper flakes and black olives. Simmer on low heat for 40 - 60 minutes. Cook the pasta 2 - 5 minutes in a large pot of boiling, salted water to which you have added a splash of olive oil. Do not overcook. Drain and toss with half of the Parmesan cheese. To serve, pour the tomato sauce over a bed of angel hair pasta and top off with the remaining Parmesan cheese.

Lemon Poppy Seed Dressing

Yields 1 cup

⅓ cup Splenda
1 tablespoon honey mustard
¼ cup red wine vinegar
¼ cup shallots, minced
2 tablespoons fresh lemon juice
Sea salt to taste
⅓ cup canola oil
4 tablespoons poppy seeds

Combine the Splenda, mustard, vinegar, shallots, lemon juice and salt in a food processor. Blend for approximately 30 - 60 seconds. Slowly pour in the canola oil while the processor is turned on. Finally, add the poppy seeds. Refrigerate and serve chilled.

Nutrition Facts
(Per Serving)

Calories	137
Fat Calories	100
Total Fat	11.1g
Saturated Fat	0.8g
Cholesterol	0mg
Sodium	82mg
Total Carbs	8.2g
Fiber	0.5g
Protein	1.1g

Did You Know…

- Onions and lemons may help protect against cancer.

Mayonnaise

Yields 1 cup

Nutrition Facts	
Serving Size: 2 Tablespoons	
Calories	75
Fat Calories	70
Total Fat	7.5g
Saturated Fat	1g
Cholesterol	26mg
Sodium	81mg
Total Carbs	0.4g
Fiber	0g
Protein	0.9g

Did You Know…

- Canola oil contains the "good" fats.
- Eggs contain choline which is essential for normal brain development. This may be of particular interest to women who are pregnant or breast feeding.
- Eggs also have been touted to enhance digestive and kidney function.

1 free range egg, whole
1 tablespoon fresh lemon juice
½ teaspoon dry mustard
Pinch of sea salt
¼ cup canola oil

Place the egg, lemon juice, mustard and salt in a food processor, and turn on the processor. Slowly drizzle in the oil until mayo thickens. Refrigerate immediately.

Sun-Dried Tomato Pesto

The pesto may be refrigerated for up to two days or frozen for one month.

1 tablespoon pine nuts
¾ cup low-fat, low-sodium organic chicken broth
½ cup sun-dried tomatoes, not in oil, coarsely chopped
3 medium cloves garlic
¼ cup Parmesan cheese, grated
½ cup lightly packed basil leaves
1 tablespoon fresh lemon juice

To toast the pine nuts, toss them in a skillet until slightly browned and fragrant.

In a small saucepan, bring the broth to a boil. Remove from the heat and add the tomatoes to the pan. Cover and let stand until the tomatoes are soft and have cooled for approximately 30 minutes. Drain, reserving 3 tablespoons of the liquid.

Place the tomatoes in a food processor. Slowly add the garlic cloves and pine nuts, and process until all of the ingredients are finely chopped. Add the cheese, basil and lemon juice. Process the mixture for about 10 seconds. Finally, add the reserved tomato liquid and process until smooth.

Yields ½ cup

Nutrition Facts

Serving Size: 2 Tablespoons

Calories 47

Fat Calories 20
Total Fat 2.2g
Saturated Fat 0.9g
Cholesterol 3mg
Sodium 244mg
Total Carbs 3.8g
Fiber 0.8g
Protein 3g

Did You Know…

- Pine nuts are high in monounsaturated fat and arginine.
- Pine nuts are also a great source of potassium and magnesium.
- Tomatoes are a good source of dietary fiber.

Sweet and Sour Sauce

Yields 1¼ cup

Nutrition Facts (Per Serving)	
Calories	86
Fat Calories	31
Total Fat	3.5g
Saturated Fat	0.4g
Cholesterol	0mg
Sodium	267mg
Total Carbs	13.1g
Fiber	0.7g
Protein	0.8g

Did You Know…

- Pineapple is an excellent source of vitamin C, manganese and vitamin B1.
- Fresh pineapple is a rich source of bromelain. Bromelain has been touted to have an anti inflammatory effect on joints within the body.
- Consuming pineapple may aid in digestion.

⅔ cup pineapple juice
¼ cup canned pineapple tidbits, drained
3 tablespoons olive oil
2 tablespoons reduced sodium soy sauce
¼ cup Splenda brown sugar
1 teaspoon of ground ginger
1 teaspoon garlic, minced
¼ cup fresh lemon juice
1 tablespoon cornstarch

Combine the pineapple juice, pineapple, oil, soy sauce, Splenda, ginger, garlic, and lemon juice into a saucepan. Heat thoroughly until sugar starts to dissolve. Add cornstarch and stir until sauce thickens. Simmer until ready to serve. For a thicker sauce, add a little more cornstarch.

Tartar Sauce with a Twist

Serves 4

- ½ cup mayonnaise
- 2 tablespoons fresh lemon juice
- 1 tablespoon prepared sweet pickle relish, drained
- 1 tablespoon capers, drained
- ½ teaspoon white pepper

Place the mayonnaise, lemon juice, pickle relish, capers and white pepper in a mixing bowl, Mix thoroughly. Serve chilled.

Nutrition Facts
(Per Serving)

Calories	126
Fat Calories	88
Total Fat	9.8g
Saturated Fat	1.5g
Cholesterol	8mg
Sodium	261mg
Total Carbs	9.2g
Fiber	0.1g
Protein	0.3g

Did You Know…

- Substituting reduced fat mayonnaise will significantly reduce the fat content of homemade tartar sauce.
- Lemons are a great source of vitamin B6, folic acid, potassium, and flavonoids.
- Lemons are an excellent source of vitamin C.

Thousand Island Dressing

Yields 1 cup

Nutrition Facts (Per Serving)	
Calories	89
Fat Calories	53
Total Fat	5.9g
Saturated Fat	1.4g
Cholesterol	7mg
Sodium	239mg
Total Carbs	7.9g
Fiber	0.2g
Protein	1g

Did You Know…

- By reducing the fat content, this traditional favorite is a healthier recipe.
- When eating salad dressing, a serving size is typically two tablespoons.

½ cup reduced fat mayonnaise
2 tablespoons blue cheese, crumbled
3 tablespoons sweet pickle relish
2 tablespoons fresh lemon juice
¼ cup ketchup
¼ teaspoon paprika
Salt to taste

Combine all the ingredients in a bowl. Mix and refrigerate. Serve chilled.

Tomato Sauce

Serves 6 - 8

28 ounces canned stewed tomatoes
16 ounces tomato sauce
6 ounces tomato paste
⅓ cup onion, diced
1 tablespoon dried oregano
1 tablespoon garlic, minced
½ teaspoon red pepper flakes
1 tablespoon olive oil
½ teaspoon Splenda
½ teaspoon salt
⅓ cup fresh basil, chopped
⅓ cup Parmesan cheese
Black cracked peppercorns to taste

Place the stewed tomatoes, tomato sauce, tomato paste, onion, oregano, garlic, red pepper flakes, olive oil, Splenda and salt in a large crock pot. Turn the crock pot on low heat. Stir to blend the ingredients. Cook on low heat for 3 hours or until ready to serve. Top off with fresh basil, cheese and pepper.

Nutrition Facts
(Per Serving)

Calories	104
Fat Calories	22
Total Fat	2.4g
Saturated Fat	0.2g
Cholesterol	0mg
Sodium	159mg
Total Carbs	17.1g
Fiber	4g
Protein	3.4g

Did You Know...

- There is five times more lycopene in tomato paste as there is in raw tomatoes.
- Combining tomatoes with olive oil can increase the absorption of lycopene.
- Basil contains two important flavonoids, orientin and vicenin. These water soluble flavonoids have been shown to protect cells from free radical damage.

Wasabi Mayonnaise

Add a little zing to your favorite sandwich.

Yields ½ cup

Nutrition Facts
(Per Serving)

Calories	60
Fat Calories	53
Total Fat	5.9g
Saturated Fat	0.7g
Cholesterol	7mg
Sodium	160 mg
Total Carbs	1.5g
Fiber	0.1g
Protein	0.1g

½ cup reduced fat mayonnaise
1½ teaspoons wasabi paste
1 teaspoon fresh lemon juice

Mix together the mayonnaise, wasabi paste and lemon juice. Combine all the ingredients in a bowl. Mix and refrigerate. Serve chilled.

Did You Know...

- Wasabi paste may have thermogenic properties as it creates heat with in the body.
- Lemons contain limonene. Limonene may help to protect against breast cancer.

desserts

Canteloupe Bowls

Serves 4

- 1 cantaloupe, halved and seeded
- 2/3 cup plain non fat organic yogurt
- 1 tablespoon Splenda brown sugar
- 1/4 teaspoon vanilla
- 1/3 cup granola, prepared (See recipe page 99)

Remove most of the flesh from the cantaloupe. Cube the flesh and place it in a mixing bowl. Gently stir in the yogurt, sugar, vanilla and granola. Place the fruit mixture inside the cantaloupe shells. Serve immediately or served chilled.

Nutrition Facts (Per Serving)	
Calories	120
Fat Calories	14
Total Fat	1.5g
Saturated Fat	0.6g
Cholesterol	2mg
Sodium	79mg
Total Carbs	22.2g
Fiber	1.7g
Protein	4.2g

Did You Know…

- Cantaloupe is rich in vitamin C, carotenes and potassium.
- The wide array of nutrients found in cantaloupe may help prevent angina attacks.
- Consuming yogurt may reduce the risk of colon cancer.

Champagne Dessert

This recipe is perfect for a bridal shower.

Serves 8

Nutrition Facts (Per Serving)	
Calories	71
Fat Calories	4
Total Fat	0.5g
Saturated Fat	0g
Cholesterol	0mg
Sodium	1mg
Total Carbs	16g
Fiber	2.3g
Protein	0.6g

2 pears, cubed
2 green apples, cubed
1 cup strawberries, sliced
1 cup mandarin oranges, segments
2 cups watermelon, cubed
¼ cup orange juice
2 tablespoon lemon juice
3 tablespoons Splenda
2 tablespoon grated orange peel
1 bottle non alcohol chilled sparkling champagne
Fresh mint to garnish

Begin by cutting a large watermelon in half. Scoop out the watermelon flesh and cube. Keep the watermelon shell for presentation purposes. In a large mixing bowl, add the watermelon, pears, apples, strawberries, oranges, orange juice, lemon juice, Splenda, orange peel, and champagne. Mix gently. Remove the ingredients form the bowl and place in the watermelon shell. Garnish with mint and serve immediately.

Did You Know...

- Watermelon is an excellent source of pure water. It also a great source of lycopene.
- Pears are a great source of pectin.
- Oranges are an excellent source of vitamin C that bolsters the immune system.

Fresh Fruit Parfait

This is an excellent choice for breakfast or a healthy snack.

6 ounces plain organic yogurt
¼ cup walnuts, chopped
1 teaspoon Splenda
¼ cup blueberries
¼ cup raspberries
¼ cup blackberries
¼ cup Kashi cereal
Strawberries or fresh mint (garnish)

Place the yogurt in a mixing bowl and blend in the Splenda. Transfer ¼ cup of the yogurt to a serving dish and begin to layer the walnuts, blueberries, raspberries and blackberries with additional layers of yogurt. Top off with the cereal and a strawberry to garnish.

Serves 6 to 8

Nutrition Facts
(Per Serving)

Calories 78
Fat Calories 36
Total Fat 3.8g
Saturated Fat 0.6g
Cholesterol 2mg
Sodium 25mg
Total Carbs 7.4g
Fiber 1.3g
Protein 3.1g

Did You Know…

- Walnuts are a rich source of Omega 3 fatty acids which are essential in our diet and cannot be made within the body.
- Blueberries are a good source of fiber, antioxidants, vitamin C and iron. They have been touted to enhance memory, and may help prevent urinary tract infections.
- Raspberries are an excellent source of vitamin C. They contain reasonable amounts of folate, iron and potassium.
- Blackberries are low in calories, high in fiber and contain large amounts of vitamin C.

Grapefruit Delite

Serves 6 to 8

Nutrition Facts (Per Serving)	
Calories	230
Fat Calories	79
Total Fat	8.8g
Saturated Fat	4.1g
Cholesterol	0mg
Sodium	43mg
Total Carbs	35mg
Fiber	3g
Protein	2.8g

Did You Know…

- Grapefruit is a great source of potassium and folic acid.
- Grapefruit also contains pectin which has been associated with reducing the risk of heart disease.
- Honey contains riboflavin and vitamin B6.

16 ounces fresh grapefruit sections
¼ cup honey
½ cup sweetened coconut
¼ cup honey roasted almonds
Fresh mint to garnish

Halve the grapefruit and scoop out the flesh. Divide the grapefruit into sections and place in a bowl. Add the honey, coconut, and almonds, and toss. Place in a parfait dish and serve chilled. Use fresh mint to garnish.

desserts

Jingle Bell Bars

Serves 8 to 10

- 1 cup flour
- 1 teaspoon baking powder
- ¾ cup white coconut or fruit of choice
- ¾ cup of a mixture of semisweet dark chocolate chips and peanut butter chips
- ⅓ cup melted butter
- ½ cup Splenda brown sugar
- ½ cup natural applesauce
- 2 egg whites
- 2 teaspoon vanilla

Preheat the oven to 325°. Combine the flour, baking powder, coconut and chips in a bowl; mix thoroughly. In a food processor, combine the butter, Splenda, applesauce, egg whites and vanilla. Pulse until blended. Add the flour mixture and pulse until blended. Spray an 8" baking pan with cooking spray. Spread the cookie dough evenly in the pan. Bake at 325° until the bars are slightly brown, approximately 40 minutes.

Nutrition Facts
(Per Serving)

Calories	122
Fat Calories	64
Total Fat	7.1g
Saturated Fat	4.5g
Cholesterol	10mg
Sodium	25mg
Total Carbs	12.5g
Fiber	0.9g
Protein	2.2g

Did You Know…

- Egg whites are a pure source of protein.
- Coconut is a good source of iron and fiber. It also is high in easy to digest fats.
- Splenda brown sugar is an excellent substitute for regular brown sugar.

Pumpkin Pudding

Serves 6

Nutrition Facts (Per Serving)	
Calories	164
Fat Calories	19
Total Fat	2.1g
Saturated Fat	0.7g
Cholesterol	71mg
Sodium	59mg
Total Carbs	30.8g
Fiber	2.7g
Protein	5.5g

Did You Know…

- Pumpkin is a type of winter squash.
- Pumpkin is a rich source of beta carotene.
- Pumpkin is a good low-calorie source of iron and potassium.
- Pumpkin is high in fiber.
- Pumpkin seeds are great toasted and are a good source of protein.

2 Freerange eggs
¾ Splenda
2 cups pumpkin purée
1 tablespoon molasses
1 teaspoon ground cinnamon
½ teaspoon ginger
¼ teaspoon ground nutmeg
¼ teaspoon ground cloves
1½ cups evaporated skim milk

Preheat the oven to 425°. Lightly coat a medium casserole dish with cooking spray. Place the eggs in a large bowl. Using an electric mixer, beat in the Splenda, pumpkin, molasses, cinnamon, ginger, nutmeg and cloves. Add the milk.

Pour the mixture in the casserole dish and bake for 10 minutes. Reduce the heat to 350° and bake for 35-40 minutes more, until the top is lightly browned and the pudding has set. Serve warm or chilled.

Notes